# YOUR MIND
# YOUR BEST FRIEND

# YOUR MIND
# YOUR BEST FRIEND

**30 Days to Build Your Most
Important Friendship**

Shuddhaanandaa Brahmachari

**Lokenath Divine Life Mission**

**Kolkata**

*For the seekers*
*in the Path of Light and Love*

# ACKNOWLEDGMENTS

I AM INDEBTED to those devotees who shared their precious time and energy in making this book possible, particularly to Ann Shannon for transcribing the original tapes and editing each edition to make it a true companion for seekers of peace and love. My special thanks, too, to Haskell Fuller for his dedication in editing this edition.

# CONTENTS

# PREFACE

Radiant Spirits and Embodiments of Pure Joy,

I have been overwhelmed by the response from readers of this gift from my heart, *Your Mind, Your Best Friend.* I have received letters from around the world about its efficacy in inspiring positive faith in one's own self and opening a simple and clearer understanding of the path of the spirit. Most people have written that they have found answers to the most unresolved questions about life and living.

To me, this indicates that the purpose of *Your Mind, Your Best Friend* is being fulfilled through the grace of the Author of authors.

My prayer is that this fourth edition will open your hearts to the simple truth that if we walk the path of meditation and a conscious life, then we come to realize that the doorway to the highest wisdom and joy lies only in one's own mind. It is not to control the mind or conquer it but to befriend the mind to transform the lower energies and vibrations to higher frequencies of eternal love and Light. A friendly mind is joyous mind.

My love and prayers for all of you for a happy journey to reach your most beloved friend in the shrine of your own heart. I am sure this book will help illumine this inner shrine of your heart and manifest as peace and humility, love and gratitude for all the invaluable, infinite gifts of the Universe.

Celebrate Life, for in essence Life is a Celebration!

Kolkata, India                              Shuddhaanandaa Brahmachari
September 2016

# FOREWORD

WHAT YOU HOLD in your hand is a spiritual gem, an un-assuming, extraordinary medium of grace and healing, a cornerstone of spiritual practice for the sincere seeker. These materials were gathered from the taped lectures of Shuddhaanandaa speaking to devotees. They come straight from the purified heart of one of God's humblest servants. Do not take my word for it. Read the first reading, do the first exercise to discover the magnitude of what awaits you.

Here, Shuddhaanandaa presents what will be a new, core concept of the life of the spirit which brings an epiphany to most readers: The mind that is your best friend, which he also terms the Befriending Mind. As Shuddhaanandaa explains and as you begin to apply the principles, it becomes readily apparent that training your mind to become your best friend, to become an ever Befriending Mind, is more than wishful thinking. It involves much more than a simplistic loyalty to being positive for its own sake or for any utilitarian benefit. It does not repress any aspect, any experience of life. The Befriending Mind which is our best friend offers a universal, grounded, and compassionate response to the deepest human suffering. It traces the root cause of suffering to its source and provides the antidote by returning to its ultimate reference point and resource: our enduring and sustaining context in a beneficent universe, in God. Taken to heart and applied, these practices begin to calm the mind of its fears, its guilt and distortions.

I speak as a devotee with 20 years of meditative practice. My practice, as it was, simply was not enough. I had always had more than a minor visceral reaction to "positive thinking." As I understood and had seen it embodied, "positive thinking" was superficial and repressive. I felt compelled to be more honest, to penetrate the deeper and harsher complexities of being human. Over the decades, however, my own approach reached its limit. My mind was collapsing in on itself. My ability to meditate, to practice at all, was withering. Rather than finding resolution and transformation, I was becoming less and less able to cope.

Mercifully, the mind responds to these truths. It responds naturally. The mind hungers for its true context. It surrenders. I cannot recommend *Your Mind, Your Best Friend* enough to you. Working with these principles and practices can free you from the past. It can sustain you through any crisis of the moment. There is no need to be dominated by any mechanism of your mind, however entrenched. There is no need to feel oppressed by yourself, by life or by circumstance. It is possible to let all of the joys and struggles of life come and go because you *know* that all is well. That possibility is not in the remote distance when you are working with these teachings.

Shuddhaanandaa is a simple monk. He is a universal spiritual teacher. His only aspiration is to serve the living God in all who suffer, to faithfully serve his Beloved. A master of himself and of devotional service to God, Shuddhaanandaa is also a master of tender and tireless compassion. He is as committed to addressing the psychological and spiritual dilemmas of the West as well as to serving the poor. We, too, suffer in the midst of abundance. Who does not suffer? What is impoverishment if not imprisonment in the illusion of our separation from God?

As Shuddhaanandaa states, we have acquired our destructive habits of mind through many years of practice. Transforming them requires effort and persistence. To ground yourself in the one, true friend of your own befriending mind, I suggest that you cycle through the readings and practices many times over. Find a pace that is workable for you. Be creative. I read from the text with a notebook, making lists of affirmations to use in my daily life. Before my husband died, he and I read the practices for each other, repeating certain phrases again and again as a part of our daily morning practice. Sometimes, a practice may bring up what stands in the way of its realization. If that happens for you as it has for us from time to time, I urge you to persist with the practice until you experience the deeper, truer reality.

Joy awaits you,
Ann Shannon, Portland, Oregon, USA
Editor

Wayfarer, there is no way
The way is made by walking
There is no way to peace and happiness
Peace and Happiness is the way

--Buddha

——— ☙❧ ———

# YOUR BEFRIENDING MIND: YOUR ONE, TRUE FRIEND

WHAT GOD WANTS of you, first and foremost, is for you to find your one true friend in the entire world. Your one true friend is your own mind which befriends you in all circumstances, a mind which always returns you to the ultimate truth of your home in the Divine. Such a mind dispels the illusion of distance and separation from God. Such a mind returns, now and here, to the living presence of the Divine in all circumstances. Such a mind is anchored in the truth of its existence in God, in the instructions of the Holy Ones, in the instruction of your master, if you have one. Your one true friend is your positive, befriending mind that is ever rooted in the realities of your oneness with the Divine.

The more committed you are to the one true friend of your befriending mind, the more your mind becomes brilliant. It becomes lustrous. It opens to consciously receive the infinite blessings that are unfolding at every instant to direct you toward the home of your own spirit, which is one with God. It opens to give you greater blessings than you ever dreamed possible.

The Enlightened Masters of the world tell us our best friend, first and foremost, must be searched for and found. So what do we do? We go about our daily lives searching, seeking a good friend for our protection, for our social living, for everything that helps us to subsist in the world. Finally, we realize it is very difficult to find a friend. After all, a friend is nothing but a mind…and a mind is the most unpredictable thing in this universe. You can never know at what moment even your best friend will suddenly turn into a hurtful stranger.

Who are we going to trust if we cannot trust our own mind? If we can't trust our own self, whom are we going to trust? The spiritual journey, thus, is always centered around our own mind, our own self, our own being. We dig in our own field to discover reality and to test it.

If you are seeking and searching for a true friend who would be by your side when you are in danger, a friend who will understand your true need, then know your mind which listens to you. Know your mind which is disciplined through yoga, meditation, prayer, and spiritual practice. Know that which allows your mind to be in Divine contemplation, to be anchored in the Divine. That kind of mind is your true friend. That kind of mind sustains you through the turbulence and vagaries of life. It doesn't allow you to drop downward because you are suddenly faced with a dire situation.

Anything can happen to you externally. External circumstances are most unpredictable. We cannot predict what is going to happen, even in the next moment. Things outside of us, people outside of us, everything that is around us is changeable, inalterably unpredictable in its nature. That is nature.

We need to find and seek a true friend in this difficult, human state.

The only real solution is to befriend yourself. Make friendship with yourself first. Then seek friends outside. When you find your mind has become your true friend, you will be surrounded with friends. You won't have enough time to see all of your friends.

When we dwell in willingness, in appreciation, in thankfulness, in trust, in true friendship with ourselves, gradually we come to realize that if whatever we are working toward, if whatever we are hoping for doesn't happen, then God is working toward some greater beneficence through whatever does happen. There is nothing to fear. There is nothing to be upset about. There is no reason to hold back from life. We move ahead freely, confidently, lovingly, befriending everybody around us, because we are befriending our own self. We never create an enemy outside, because we never live with the enemy inside.

In that state of friendliness within, you are never a victim. There is no self-condemnation, there is no guilt, there is no question of blame, there is no depression. Your mind is more and more vibrant. It is buoyant. It moves naturally upward because it is light. It vibrates at a very high level. It attracts the ethereal vibrations of the holy saints and sages that are eternally available to all human beings throughout the ages. The words of the saints and sages, their inspiration, their grace flows out to you. Everything is available to you the moment you raise your mind and heart to that positive field. Ever so gradually, you absorb the graceful teachings of the Lord. You grasp new, deeper meanings. You grow in awareness and consciousness. You come to understand the essence, you become the essence, of the eternal teachings.

# PRACTICE

Spend some time before the mirror, looking into your own eyes. Affirm that you are a radiant child of eternal light. See the beauty, the goodness, the Divine love shining in your own eyes. Remind yourself that you come from God, that you are showered in God's love, that you share that Divine love with everyone you meet, that you love yourself, and that others love you. Know that you are a blessing to your family and to society. Feel the glow of Divine grace and love in your own heart. Work on the plane of spiritual consciousness as well as on the physical plane. Look into your eyes without blinking and feel the calmness there. Recognize the blessings of God manifesting in your being.

Doing this mirror work regularly will make you more beautiful. It will create miracles. You will grow in self-esteem. You will become more aware of your inner strength and power of mind. Divine grace will manifest miracle after miracle around you. You will become your own, true, orienting center.

# THE UNIVERSAL JOURNEY

OUR HUMAN JOURNEY is from lower truth to higher truth, from darkness and ignorance to light and wisdom, from fear of death to deathlessness. It is a journey through the mind, a journey which trains the mind, a journey which always returns the mind to its true, encompassing home in the unifying spirit. We do the basic work of that journey by continuously cultivating our befriending mind, anchoring and re-anchoring ourselves in the ultimate truths of spirit.

We all have God in our hearts. However, God in one who is awakened is alive, fully conscious and available. That is why so many of us worship enlightened masters. We honor the Divine they have mastered and which they embody, because deep in our hearts, in the very core of our being, God is. God lives within us. God is our own Beloved.

The extent to which we feel the presence of the Divine, the extent to which we see the world through the eyes of our innate divinity, makes all the difference. It is nothing but a notion of our minds that God is somewhere else — in the heavens, deep in the clouds, far, far away from us — and that we need to call God to come to us, to bless us, and rid us of our troubles.

God is nowhere else. God is now and here. If you could squeeze all the religions of the world into one drop of wisdom, it would be: God is now and here...nowhere else.

The function of all religion and all spirituality is to bridge the gap between the seeker, the Enlightened Ones, and God.

No one creates this distance but us. The distance, the separation between us and God, is an illusion of the mind. That illusion may be stubborn. That illusion may be convincing. It is also the source of all human misery, so penetrating the illusion each and every time it arises is a central, critically important practice of the sincere devotee.

We ourselves create the distance of our separation from God. That core illusion veils our consciousness like a darkened shroud. We are also the only ones who can dispel that shadow.

The human mind is conditioned by eons of inherited patterns of perception and response, by our personal, existential ethos — those sets of attitudes and beliefs, or *samskaras* that support survival in a given environment. All of these impressions are buried deep in the multiple layers of our subconscious mind. It takes time, perseverance, faith, inordinate compassion and commitment, to uproot and weed them all out.

Self-awareness is the ancient, yogic path to liberation. Our minds are only marginally aware of ourselves. Through yoga, we collect ourselves, we return to now and here. Yoga brings us here, right now, to our experience at this instant, so that you are nowhere else.

We cannot climb a mountain to reach God. We cannot walk a hundred or even a thousand miles to reach God. We cannot go to a church, mosque, or temple to reach God. We cannot go to the forest to find God. God can only be found in the truth of nearness. God is within us all.

That is the message of the Vedas, the most ancient wisdom of the world's spiritual literature. You are the children of immortality. You are inseparable from the Ultimate Reality. You and Reality are One. You are indivisible from all that is. This is the *Dharma* of mankind.

Thus, we are blessed. We are blessed by all of the Great Ones who have gone before us. We are blessed by each instant, by each experience of our lives, leading us certainly and ultimately home. We know that. We always knew.

The guru, the teacher and guide of the soul, comes only to confirm it, to reaffirm it, to hammer the nail again so that it goes a little deeper, so that faith deepens, so that trust happens. We learn to move with trust, with faith, from head to the heart, and to open our heart with single-pointed devotion. With love, befriending ourselves and all whom we meet, we move toward that one, encompassing reality, toward that One Truth, toward "The One Without the Second" spoken of in Vedic tradition.

# PRACTICE

Spend some time reflecting and writing on the process of your own unfolding. Look back over your own life's journey. Trace the major threads and themes of the evolution of your spirit from childhood until today. What have the driving forces been to your personal evolution of consciousness? How has your life been a movement from the lower to the higher, from darkness to light, from fear to faith? How have any experiences of your own lower nature, of darkness, of fear and pain, ultimately contributed to your turning more to the life of your spirit? What still burdens you today? If those burdens were lifted, what would you have gained from having them? Then reflect on the larger journey of human evolution in the same way. How are we all on a collective journey?

# LIFT YOUR MIND WITH YOUR OWN MIND

YOUR MIND IS the thing with which you are working, either to lower yourself or to uplift yourself, whether to bind yourself or to free yourself. All miseries come from the bondage of the untrained mind.

God knows fully well that we are all entrapped by the creations of our own mind...that we are all entangled by our own *mayic* illusions... that we all are trapped in our projected thoughts, ideas, and concepts. God knows how human it is to fall prey to the games of mind, to fall into self-deception.

A truly spiritual mind is always positive. A truly spiritual mind is a controlled mind. One of the ways by which you can control your mind is to lift your mind with your own mind. Uplift yourself by yourself. Free yourself. Unfetter and unchain yourself. It is the mind which is in bondage. It is the mind which can unfetter and free itself. Lift yourself up.

Lift to the higher realms of the spirit within you. That is the gateway to peace and happiness.

The ultimate state of human mind occurs when the mind becomes single-pointed and flows uninterruptedly toward its own origin in spirit, toward its intrinsic Divine potential.

That positive, befriending mind is the greatest blessing to an individual.

The blessing is not only to the individual, however. It is a blessing for all humanity, for the whole universe.

The positive, befriending mind is in a state of continuous, authentic celebration. It is ever in the present, ever celebrating the presence of the Divine.

Our positive, befriending mind is a mind that looks for the blessing hands of the Lord behind all that is transient in nature.

It sees the sun beyond the clouds of circumstance.

Our positive, befriending mind is a state of yoga in the truest sense. It yokes us, uniting us with the field of our communion with the indestructible Beloved, with that which is beyond fear, beyond anxieties, beyond all troubles and tribulations, beyond all negativity.

Our positive, befriending mind is the mind at peace with itself, at one with the world around it. Cultivating our positive, befriending mind is the basic, essential spiritual practice without which all other practice falls short.

We can all cultivate a positive, befriending mind. It is a gift we can give to our family, one we can give to our friends, one we can give to our co-workers. We can give our positive, befriending mind to the entire universe. There is no greater gift.

# PRACTICE

When you find yourself facing any difficult or painful situation, practice asking yourself, "What deeper good might God be working toward here? What might my spirit be growing toward through this? How can I open my mind and heart and spirit to give consent to the Divine's purposes, however hidden they may be from my current understanding?" There is no need to come up with "answers" *per se*. Rather, hold the questions prayerfully in your heart, resolving to remain open and accepting, with a willingness to receive insight into the deeper mysteries at work in even the most difficult circumstances.

# BECOMING A PATIENT AND LOVING GUIDE TO YOUR OWN MIND

LIKE A LOVING and watchful parent, the sincere devotee gradually learns to guide the mind, to monitor its straying, to redirect it. The essential practice is this: to patiently and firmly turn the mind away from all illusion of negativity toward home, toward what is eternally real and ultimately true in the spirit.

Gradually, we learn: never, ever allow the mind to droop. If we do, it snowballs. It goes into a downward spiral. We need always to be alert. We need always to be awake. We need always to be open and watchful of the thoughts of the mind, observing how the mind plays, where it goes, of its own accord. We need always to cultivate our befriending mind.

Most of us are not alert. We don't know or notice when the negative forces start to play. Often, it is only when we are in the abyss that we begin to realize it. Then it is very difficult to pull back, to reverse direction.

If only we could always be meditative, prayerful, in touch with the guru, in touch with our Beloved, the Beloved within! If only we could stay in touch with the remembrance of the Divine Name within, continuously praying for the support of Divine grace, continuously praying for Divine love's protection! Then it is Divine grace, it is Divine love that manifests as conscious awareness of our mind. We are watchful. We are vigilant. We are keen to know what our mind is saying, where it is leading us. Then, we do not allow our mind to become depressed, to get mired in untruth and spin out of control, to be an undisciplined child who does not listen to us.

# PRACTICE

Whenever you notice yourself falling into self-criticism, catch yourself. Befriend yourself. Remind yourself; to fall in your own self-esteem is to fall into an abyss.

You are on a journey home to your true Self, to who you are in God. The vehicle of your mind naturally veers off course from time to time. You notice when it is leaving the highway, when it is taking you on a detour by falling into negativity. You simply make an adjustment by steering your mind back to the highway of what is true. Redirect your mind by recalling all the ways in which the Divine tenderly, intimately, and actively loves you. Think of all the ways grace has moved through your life. See your heart and mind being washed in Divine light and grace until you know, again, who you are in God.

Recall the ways you serve others, the ways in which you work to manifest Divine love and compassion, and know that God is within you. Affirm the beauty of your spirit as the truth of who you are.

Affirm that the good in you is infinitely stronger, more powerful, and enduring than any conditioned, transient, human limitation. Know that all limitations will ultimately fall away to reveal the truth of the Divine spirit, whose home is your heart. Bless others on their journey, and cultivate compassion for all the ways in which we lose our way. Rejoice in the goodness that flows through your life, and every human life, despite our illusory human limitations, and release all imperfection to the tender mercy and love of God for transformation.

# ATTENDING THE LIGHT WITHIN

THERE IS A single web of mind, One Cosmic Mind within which we are all living and evolving. If I am not able to be conscious of the vast, Infinite Cosmic Mind, that is no problem. I do not have to worry about that. I may not know what is in the mind of God, but I can become conscious and aware of what is in my mind! I can reflect upon my own mind. I can see my own mind. I can watch my own mind, rather than letting it play itself out unconsciously.

That attentive quality of consciousness, that awareness, is a kind of lamp which burns. In India, we say that temple looks best where there is a light continuously burning, enlightening the beautiful face of the Lord. We never allow that light to be extinguished.

We need the lamp in the temple, but we also need the lamp that burns ceaselessly within. The temple priest must be careful and watchful to see that the oil does not run out.

He replenishes the oil. He trims the wick to the right length to keep the light burning. It takes watchfulness, alertness to keep the lamp in the temple burning. The lamp within needs our watchful mind to tend the flame that is burning in our heart.

The lamp is the flame of our aspiration. It is our yearning, our love for truth, our love for all that is good and beautiful, our love for God, our love of knowing our own Self. It is our love of knowing who we are, why we are, where we are. Every fundamental question comes to be addressed, comes to resolution, provided we try to see through the lamp in our own heart and give up borrowing the answers of others.

That is the light of awareness that we need to keep aflame in our hearts. Those who have that lamp, that awareness, ever burning in their heart, never go wrong in that light. They befriend everything that comes to them. They read between the lines. They come to understand the language by which God is trying to communicate to them. Such a mind is truly devoted, dedicated, offered to the Divine. Such a mind gradually gets purified and is refined until it becomes stainless once again.

## PRACTICE

As part of your morning prayers, spend some time writing or thinking about your deepest aspirations and longings for the coming day. Then spend 10 minutes in the evening writing about what uplifted your life and spirit throughout the day. What moments of inspiration and insight, beauty and light, peace and joy were there? What moments of human strength, courage, or tenderness were you privileged to witness or give? What kindled the ever-burning lamp of awareness in your heart? Let your heart wash a little deeper in the grace of those gifts. Make it a practice to gather the gifts of the day, to savor them in your heart, to thank God for them each night before going to bed.

# AS YOU THINK, SO YOU BECOME

YOUR BEFRIENDING STATE of mind will attract the positive to you. As the seers of India often say, *"Yadrishi bhavana yashya siddhir bhavati tadrishihi."* As you think so you become. Whatever your thought, whatever your continuous thoughts, accordingly, you become that.

A truly happy person is one who continually dwells upon the thought of God. He or she is continually dwelling on the thought of God, the Divine play of God, the words of God, God's grace, God's presence in everything, every moment. Such a person sees the Divine hand in everything.

Life is very simple. The best friend is one's own mind. There is no need to seek outward support anymore. Support comes from inside. It is like a fountain that was just emptied. Its source is open, so the waters come flooding back in.

We create our own heaven and we live in that heaven. We create our own hell and we live in that hell.

If you live in hell in this world, in this physical body, know there is another hell waiting for you when you leave this body. It will follow you wherever you go. Because you created a hell for yourself, you framed a hell that is going to go with you.

Whatever the last thought you have in your mind, accordingly, you find your home in the astral plane. The last thought, does not come by accident. It comes from the accumulations of the past, reaching forward to form the present. The whole of the past goes to meet the last moment.

Why do we need to be prayerful always, watchful always, aware always? So we will not forget reality. Then we do not cheat ourselves or anyone else. Then, at our last moment, when there can be no cheating, at that moment when you are naked to your own self, where you cannot hide anymore, you are absolutely open to your true Self. If you have practiced cultivating your positive, befriending mind for a long time, if your mind is ever in Divine love, obviously, in that last moment you will have the thought of God and nothing else. Your movement will be toward God because you have been nurturing thoughts of God throughout your lifetime.

If you continuously practice negative thoughts, that take you away from truth. If you practice warring, you basically war with yourself. You are fighting yourself. You are draining your own energy.

If you are cursing your fate, that you had this or that bad friend, that someone has caused you a bad experience, you are only cursing yourself. Look up. There is no enemy outside! Your only enemy resides in you! Your only enemy is inside you! That enemy is your uncontrolled state of mind.

Your enemy is your own mind in ignorance of the relationship of the mind that is individual with the mind that is universal.

Your enemy is your mind that is small, without understanding of its oneness with the mind that is infinite. Such a mind cannot connect between the two, so it has a very small supply of energy. Its reference point is very small, very shallow: the ego.

Anyone can throw negative at you. Whether you accept it or not depends on your readiness. Nobody should be able to catch you unaware. You can move with awareness. You can think with awareness. You can breathe with awareness. You can see with awareness. You can respond with awareness. You can always be conscious of the inner thinker, seer, walker. It is a question of gradual practice. It is a question of living in a state of friendship, of awareness rather than ignorance or self-forgetfulness.

You cannot escape the law of the universe: whatever you give will come back to you. Give positive, positive comes back to you. Give negativity, negative comes back to you. It is a cycle. It is up to us to anchor ourselves in the firm conviction, in the faith that, yes, we are not going to move an inch, we are not going to budge, even a little, from our commitment and dedication to our own faith in our oneness with God.

# PRACTICE

We begin by keenly watching our mind. That is the true meditation of *Raja Yoga*. If we truly want to take care of the difficult clingings of our mind, then we must watch our mind. We become very conscious. We become alert to the ways and directions in which the mind pulls us. We intervene. We adjust. We compassionately guide the course of the mind to higher ground whenever it begins to slip toward negativity, knowing that if the mind ever gets caught up in the negative, it pulls us down with the certainty of gravity.

Take a few moments several times each day to keenly observe your thoughts. Observe when things are going well. Also observe when things are going badly. What specific thoughts are you having? What are you saying to yourself about what is happening? Think back to when this particular pattern of thinking and feeling began. Was it stimulated by a particular event, by something that reminded you of the past? Does the pattern itself have its roots in childhood, in your relationship with your parents? Notice the energy, the feelings, the attitudes, the sense of possibility or lack of possibility that your thoughts stimulate, reinforce, deepen and intensify. Notice the conclusions you draw, the actions which your pattern of thinking promotes, the responses those actions evoke from others. Notice how all of that combines to sustain a given direction of feeling, thinking, possibility, and response. Then ask yourself, "Is this leading me where I really want to go?" If it does, offer gratitude to God for the grace in that. If it is not, do not condemn or belittle yourself. That only leads you from darkness to deeper darkness.

To err is human. To recognize a mistake and invoke the power and grace of God to correct it is *sadhana*, spiritual practice.

As you recognize a mistake, decide to change, and open your heart to God's grace, things begin to change naturally. They happen subtly. There is no need to force yourself if change is not immediately apparent. You and God are working together now. Relax and let go of the mind. Allow the mind to settle. As it settles, you feel calm. As you calm down, you feel peace within and grace can work more effectively through you.

# UNHAPPINESS AS A CONTRACT

THE MORE YOU practice cultivating your befriending mind, nobody can make you unhappy unless you resolve to be unhappy. No outside circumstances, no situation can make you unhappy unless you agree to become unhappy, unless you sign the contract to be unhappy.

There is a contract to be unhappy. There is an offer and there is an acceptance. Then it becomes a contract. Somebody may make you an offer, but if you reject it, there is no contract. It is up to us with any external, negative situation. Until we sign, there is no contract. It cannot bind us. We are free. We need to be certain that we understand the terms of the agreement. Take the time to be sure. Don't sign until you know what you are agreeing to creates a bond of friendliness. The bond of friendliness comes only when you sign with full awareness, knowing that you are befriending your own mind, knowing that you are truly acting on your own behalf, on behalf of your spirit.

# PRACTICE

Deeply contemplate the above. Realize the truth in it. Understanding is important. Understanding triumphs over conflict and confusion. You are one step up on the ladder of *sadhana*. You can give up any deep-seated resentment or negative clinging of the mind the instant you understand that the time to correct the situation is now and here.

Resolve to give up brooding over any negative contracts of the past. Whatever happened was necessary to free your soul of your past debts. Who can pay our debts but us? We cannot escape the law of *karma*. Relax. Thank God and yourself that you have paid a debt that owed. Now it is time to shake off any clinging to the pain. Start consciously blessing all who bring pain into your life.

They are your true friends who humble you, who soften you, who till the soil in which you can forever bind yourself to God.

You have signed a new contract with God. Now you belong to the Universe alone. It is time for true celebration. Celebrate with the Universe in its unending dance of life and be happy!

# YOU HAVE ONLY ONE FRIEND AND NO ENEMIES

You HAVE NO friend or enemy outside of you. If you think deeply about it, you will find that you have only one friend and no enemies. If there is an enemy, take care of it. You take care of it by being positively oriented within your own mind. Continuous prayer, continuous meditation, continuous dwelling with those higher thoughts will gradually release the potential Divine powers within you. That gradually elevates you to a plane where negativity cannot reach you.

Positive power is within us. Negative power is within us. What we accept is up to us. There is no satisfaction in finding anybody else responsible for the miseries of our lives. That only increases the burden of our misery.

You have come to this body with the accumulated *karma* of your past and past lives. You have come to this life to work out this backlog. Do not add any more than what is to be burned in this life. It is not intelligent to add to it with further negativity.

The more you resist and react to what has come to you, the more it persists, the more it lingers, the more it increases.

In India, the story is told of a bicycle thief who once stood before the judge to receive his punishment. The judge asked the thief, "Did you steal the bicycle?" The thief replied, "No sir, I did not". The judge said, "Pay 10 rupees and go." The thief further pleaded, "Sir, I am a very poor man. I can't afford a penny. How can I pay 10 rupees?" The judge said, "Pay 20 rupees and go". The thief continued to insist that he be allowed to go without any penalty. The judge replied, "Pay 50 rupees and go". The thief pleaded, "Sir, I will die. I can never pay that. Please forgive me". The judge said firmly and calmly, "Pay 100 rupees and go!" The thief finally had to pay 100 rupees to be free.

This is a story about our destiny, created by none but ourselves in ignorance.

When you can be released by paying only 10 rupees, why pay 100? Everything that happens on the mental or physical plane happens due to our past karmic debts. If we pay our debts without grumbling, without further negativity, they are soon cleared.

Witness the inevitabilities of life as they come and go. Don't grumble over them. Allow the clouds to pass away, with your mind fixed on the sun of awareness of God's grace and light. Allow God's grace to work on any negative forces. Then, you find life is full of ease. You allow God to take care of you. You allow your godly mind to take care of you. You allow your Divine potential to take care of you. Thus, you have your best friend along with you everywhere you go in the world.

In such state of mind, you are a renunciate monk. You may be wearing any clothes of your choice, but your state of mind is the mind of a true monk, never reactive, ever responsive. A true seeker's mind is dwelling on the plane of that positive, one-pointed thought of the Divine potential that is within, on grace and its manifestations. Then continuously, acceptance happens. It happens spontaneously.

That is what we all are seeking in life. It is the one thing we need to achieve. It is important that we always return to a positive frame of mind. Never look through the glasses of negativity. Never analyse anything from a negative frame. See the hands of the Divine behind every small instance in your life, however bitter or sweet. Convert any situation into your favor, by changing your attitude toward that situation.

# PRACTICE
Before falling asleep at night, affirm:

I am a child of Immortal Bliss and Peace. All *karma* is being burned in the fire of my illumined Mind. The foundation of joy is springing forth from within me to flood my body and mind and to spill out into the world. I am in perfect celebration with all of Creation and at rest in Mother Nature.

When you awaken each morning, take some time to be conscious of the reality that you are passing from one state of consciousness to the other, from a sleeping state to the awakened state. This is an exercise in awareness of your true awakening.

Smile to yourself. Greet the morning with a smile. Tell yourself:

I am blessed to see this beautiful morning, which is fresh and new. I come to this present moment only to greet its freshness in my body and mind. I am grateful to Mother Nature for healing me, for renewing and releasing all that is old in my body and mind as I sleep. I am healthy. I know success will greet me as I move from moment to moment during the course of the day, anchored in the joy of my spirit. The joy within my spirit will touch everybody I meet today, adding to the love and peace in their lives. I feel peace in my body, in my mind, and in everything around me. All is well.

# PRACTICING PRAYER AND COMPASSION FOR OTHERS WHO ARE NEGATIVE

THE MORE WE focus on any situation with a positive, be-friending mind, the more the light within enlightens our inner temple. Darkness flees away. The more anyone attacks you with negativity, the more you should grow in awareness and consciousness. Fill that person with the positive vibrations of your heart, with compassion, with love. Fill your own heart with prayers for that person and for your own limitations in forgiveness, compassion, and understanding.

We support a person who is physically disabled. Our heart melts, our heart aches, for anyone who is mentally disabled. We need just as much compassion for anyone in a negative frame of mind. We might know fully well that a person is negative. As a truly good human being, as a conscious human being, however, we will not further bombard or burden that person with any negative thoughts or energy from us. As a good human being, we know that everyone has good in them if we look a little deeper, so we reinforce that good.

When we add to the negative burden anyone carries, we are damaging that person. We are damaging the whole environment. We are polluting the environment and we will be condemned to the consequences of that. We will pay a price for it, for we are a part of the pollution of the planet.

If we are truly conscious, we pray for those around us who are negative rather than condemning them. We bless them rather than obsessing on a desire for revenge, or getting stuck in any wound we feel they caused us. We uplift ourselves, we uplift them, we uplift the world with our sincere prayers for their healing and our own, whatever wrong we may feel has been done to us.

This is a very important spiritual practice because, in fact, no wrong has been done to us. We have simply paid an unpleasant *karmic* debt and we have been offered a spiritual opportunity in the process. When we offer our human suffering to God and find the blessing in it, we have moved along in our spiritual journey. We are one step closer to union with God and we have brought the world one step closer to that day when others will do the same. There can be no grief in that, no regret in that. There is only cause for joy in the triumph of the spirit over this little bit of darkness which God has seen fit to give us to wrestle with and transform.

# PRACTICE

Whenever you feel injured or wounded by another and you find yourself brooding over how wronged you feel and their fault in the matter, turn your mind to prayer. See yourself, the other person, and the situation held in a field of Divine light. See the light flowing into your heart and mind, into their heart and mind, to resolve the situation in Divine time. As you both fill with healing light, know that you are loved. Know that they are loved. Know that you are safe. Know that they are safe. Know that you have nothing to fear or to be angry about. Bless the other person. Ask God to illuminate the mind and heart of everyone involved, to lead you all to the highest ground possible from which to view the situation. Pray for the strength and wisdom to truly accept the other person as they are, and to hold them in a heart of compassion. Ask if there is anything you can do to heal the situation. If there is, do it with detachment, without expectation, releasing the outcome to God.

# OVERCOMING THE FIVE AFFLICTIONS OF THE MIND

THE WHOLE PURPOSE of spiritual discipline is to return our own mind to its stainless, innocent, pristine state. All Enlightened Masters tell us, "You have no problem other than your impure mind." It is only in the clouded state of impurity that you lose your true vision. Your vision is clouded by the five afflictions of mind which were described by the great, ancient scientist of life, Rishi Patanjali.

All humans are affected by the five afflictions. These five afflictions are the cause of all human miseries on this planet. They all occur because we allow our minds to droop, to go into negative fields, unaware. In our unconsciousness, we are unable to catch the mind when it is about to droop. In a person who is not aware, who is not conscious, who is not alert, and whose lamp is not burning, 'ignorance', the first affliction, takes root in the mind. 'Ego', the second affliction, then manifests itself. The other three afflictions that follow are 'attachment', the third affliction, 'repulsion', the fourth affliction, and, in the extreme case, an intense 'fear of death', which is the fifth affliction.

Ignorance is a state of Self-forgetfulness. When we are unaware, when we are unconscious, we enter the state of ignorance. We are detached from our spiritual being, from our spiritual Self. We are attached instead to our body, to our mind, to our intellect in its impure identification. Our mind becomes clouded with ignorance. We start accepting that which is false as true. We start accepting that which is unreal as real. In that state of mind, we cannot penetrate below the skin in our perception or understanding.

There is an ancient story in India of King Janaka, when he called multitudes of sages and saints to his court. He wanted to have the supreme knowledge of the Self, to learn the wisdom of God from them. The court was open; conversations were underway, when suddenly the great Sage of that time entered. Everybody started laughing loudly. Sage Ashtavakra's body was that of a cartoon figure, bent in eight places. He looked very strange, so everyone laughed.

When Ashtavakra laughed louder than all the others, the court fell into stunned silence. King Janaka immediately invited Ashtavakra to sit on his seat. Janaka washed Ashtavakra's feet and said, "Master, I have a question. I can understand why all of these people are laughing, but I don't understand why you are laughing louder than anyone else".

Sage Ashtavakra answered, "Janaka, I thought you were a very intelligent person. I never knew that you were a fool." Janaka responded, "How strange! Why? What wrong have I done?" Ashtavakra replied, "You have invited all of the cobblers to your court in order to learn the highest wisdom of God from them. They are worthy to only take care of shoes".

When the saintly king asked him to further elaborate, Ashtavakra said, "Those who can only see the skin, those whose vision is only skin deep, how could they ever see the spirit within, the essence within, the Self within, the God within, the pure Mind within? Obviously, I can't take them to be wise. I was laughing to think that you have invited all of these people to give you the supreme knowledge of the Self".

Most of our knowledge is skin deep. We cannot see beyond the skin. When we see only the skin, we judge with the yardstick of our shallow perception, with the narrow and false identifications of the ego. Through the spectacles of the false ego, we see everything as it appears. That is never the reality. Our vision is only skin deep. Ignorance leads to ego. Egotism is nothing but a cloud; it never allows us to see reality. Wherever there is false identification, the grossness of the energy and consciousness manifests as exaggerated body consciousness.

# PRACTICE

Compassionately observe the ways in which you identify with your limitations, the ways in which you feel defined by your failures, the ways in which you feel condemned to live out the patterns of the past. Notice what you say to yourself inwardly about such things. Counter every false statement with a true one. For example: In response to, "I have tried so many times to change this habit unsuccessfully – I am hopeless," tell yourself something like, "This may be an old and stubborn pattern, but it is nothing in comparison to the power of God, the masters, and my Spiritual teacher to transform it. This problem is not my enemy. It is an occasion for grace, a friend of my soul that offers me the chance to draw closer than ever to God."

Then take time in your daily prayers to sit quietly, holding this and any other patterns you seek to overcome up to the light of God's mercy and love. Trust in your will power, in concert with the Will of God, to set anything right in your life. Rest in the certainty that the process of true transformation has begun.

# TRANSFORMING WORDLY ATTACHMENTS

INVARIABLY THE DEPTH of worldly attraction and attachment takes deep root in the subconscious layers of the mind. Each of us develops our own preferences and priorities. When those preferences and priorities are violated, violence can erupt at any moment.

Attachment can be external or internal. The attachment to certain people, to certain situations, outcomes and objects, of course, is external. It can also be internal, the inner attachment to certain thoughts, concepts, ideas, philosophies and ideologies.

Attachment conditions your mind. It grips your mind tightly. It is difficult to get away from its clutch. You cling to your concepts, your ideas. Your thoughts become a condition, a film on your mind. This thick coating that never allows the mind to see with its natural brilliance. The mind cannot shine as a clear, clean space that is without contamination or coloration.

Your ego is the foundation of attachment. It is the basis of all worldliness. You feed your attachments; you multiply them without knowing it. That which you desire causes things to happen. The universe, however, has its own sublime teaching methods.

Whatever you are attached to, that is the place from which the blows of your life will come. We are all enrolled in the university of life. Whether we realize it or not, we are constantly being groomed. We are being taught at every moment. The instant we get caught up in worldly attachments, the moment we cling to something, we attach our own concepts, our ideas, our thoughts, our philosophies to it. We won't be shaken from it. That clinging immediately results in a miserable state of mind. It is a negative force. With a force akin to gravity, it instantly begins to attract blows from outside. Then we have our lesson.

Material attachment, however, prepares the ground for a higher life, the life of Divine attachment. If you have not realized the futility, the fragility and pain involved in materialistic attachments, you do not graduate to the higher realms of Divine love. Divine love is the unconditional love which is the foundation of the universe. It alone paves the way for true freedom from all forms of bondage and agony.

God wants our love. The universe longs for it. Until attachment is transmuted into Divine ecstasy, you can never be free.

Where there is attachment, its opposite is also present: rejection and repulsion. If you are attached to something, you are inevitably going to receive a blow in relation to it. That is a given. Then you are going to be filled with that irritable state of your mind which rejects and is repulsed. You reject the blow. You object to and are repulsed by all that is counter to that to which you have become identified and attached.

Attraction and repulsion are bi-polar manifestations of the mind. They continuously pull us back and forth, from one side to the other, like a pendulum. We all swing between the two extremes of these manifestations. Go through the book of your own life to see the truth of this. The source of your greatest happiness has also been the source of your deepest insecurity and unhappiness.

When the mind is allowed to play of its own accord between these fields, we are not really conscious. Control of the mind becomes difficult. Without proper training to control the mind, anything that happens can rob the mind of its higher properties, the stable state of equanimity. If we allow the intensifying energies of the mind in attachment and the lower, debasing energies of the mind to play freely, havoc rules.

In our childhood days, we played with certain toys. We were attracted to them. We were attached to our toys. The time ultimately comes, however, when we throw all attachments away, like the toys of childhood. We no longer need them. The attachment has disappeared. We no longer have the mind for them because we have grown toward something else, something more appropriate to where we are today.

The need is to practice living in a state of God consciousness rather than ego consciousness. We need to practice living in a state of Divine love rather than mere attachment to the physical or superficial. We need to practice living in the state of love and compassion rather than hatred toward others. Without love and devotion, no spiritual practice can find fulfilment. Of particular importance is being conscious of not nurturing any ill-feeling toward any member of your own family, however negative someone might be.

# PRACTICE

Observe how attachment manifests in your life. What upsets you? What makes you anxious? When do you behave other than in ways you aspire to? Ask yourself what attachments and expectations are underlying to your upsets and behaviours. How are you being affected by your attachments? How are others affected by your attachments? What tolerance and resignation, what unconsciousness, what misery has accumulated in your life as a result of these attachments? Then include time in your prayers each day to sit quietly, holding those attachments in the light of God's mercy and love, asking God to show you the path to liberation, to ever deeper devotion and conscious commitment to your spirit. Lay the matter at the feet of the Divine, resting in your trust that the transformation has begun. Cultivate conscious awareness of the play between these poles. That makes it difficult for the thieves of lower mind to break into your house and rob the precious treasures of peace and harmony in your family and home.

# OVERCOMING FEAR OF DEATH

THE FIFTH AFFLICTION according to Patanjali is too much desire for life; too much clinging to life; too much attachment to the body, its senses, and all that the senses give. Out of this comes tremendous fear of death.

Some people are haunted by the fear of death. Out of that fear comes a jungle state, a chaotic state of mind. They fall into depression. They cannot listen to the words of the Lord.

To be positively conscious is simple. It is to be positively aware that everything that happens in our life happens for a purpose. Nothing can happen out of sheer coincidence. Nothing is an accident. What happens has to happen. There is a purpose. We discover the purpose by practicing the art of reading between the lines. We can only read between the lines with eyes that are wide open. Our eyes are not just physical eyes. We cultivate awareness, the eyes of higher levels of thought, vibration, and watchfulness.

Such persons grow in awareness and consciousness. They move to higher planes where no negativity can touch them, where no attachment can possess them, where no ego can overpower them. Ignorance is driven away because they have the lamp of awareness ever burning in their heart, enlightening the mind. Now, the mind sees through the light of God.

By awareness, we mean the light of God. These particular, small eyes of the individual are no longer the ones that are seeing. The positive, befriending mind is seeing. That controlled, friendly mind is seeing. When you see through a friend's eyes, everything is friendly and good.

When we start worshipping the Divine and opening our heart in prayer, we begin to continuously expand. In that expansion, all of the constrictions, all of the narrow energy within us, and all of the consciousness begins to move, to flow. We are working to open the floodgates, to allow our conscious connection to the Divine to happen spontaneously.

Those who are blessed with a positive state of mind, those who are doing *sadhana* to attain a positive state of mind, can do and undo things by sheer will. They can do great things in this world. With their positive power of mind, they can influence any number of minds because they have befriended their own mind.

So the most important task in life, the greatest achievement, is to seek the true friend. Our best friend is our positive mind. Our worst enemy is our negative state of mind. The choice is ours. These words of wisdom are given to us by those who have practiced it and found the way to peace and happiness. We also are given the choice. We choose. It is up to us. Do we choose the friend, or do we choose to have the enemy with us? There is no use in condemning anyone else, for if you condemn, you shall be condemned.

# PRACTICE

To practice developing a positive, befriending mind, sit in meditation. Open yourself to the Divine Presence. See yourself encircled by the light of the Divine. Know that light is always protecting you, always guiding you, always informing you, always uplifting you. See Divine light forming a protective shield around you, a shield which allows no negative to penetrate. See yourself moving through the coming day within this circle of Divine light. Surrender any negative that comes to you, any negative that arises within you, into the light. Feel it being burned away. Feel the joy in that. Feel yourself returned to an ever deepening awareness of this one, ultimate reality: you belong to the Divine; you are held in an eternal circle of divine light; you walk in a universe of Divine love. You stand forever in the circle of Divine energy. Affirm your willingness to learn from every life experience and to gain the full measure of its contribution to your soul's consciousness.

Practice this meditation any time you find yourself bombarded with negative from within or without. Simply step back in your heart, in your mind's eye, into that circle of light, knowing it will lead you to true understanding.

Resolve to redirect every negative thought by holding it, and the situation that gives rise to it, in the light. Be assured, your devotion to God's light and love will take care of all the negativity. You will be in the body, yet free, celebrating moment to moment.

# PRACTICING DETACHMENT: OFFERING ALL OUTCOMES TO THE DIVINE

How DO WE gain release from the stubborn grip of attachment?

We begin with keen awareness of the anxiety, the misery our attachment causes, not only to ourselves, but also to those around us, to those we love. We begin to see how all attachment robs us of peace of mind. Then we begin to understand the importance of letting go. We begin to practice letting go.

The instant we realize we are in attachment to a certain outcome, we let go of our demand that life fit our limited expectations. We let go of our demand for a certain outcome. Every time we begin the day, every time we begin a new activity, we humbly dedicate it to God. We lovingly release the outcome to God. We open our hearts to grace, willing to become the instrument of God's purposes. We simply do what we do as a servant, as a prayer, in self-offering. We do what we do for its own sake, utterly surrendering the outcome to God.

A beautiful story is told of Buddha and Ananda. They were travelling together. Suddenly Buddha said, "I am thirsty. I want a little water to drink." Ananda remembered that when they were coming through the village they saw a small stream. So Ananda thought, "Let me go there for some water". He ran to the stream but, just as he got there, a bullock cart had passed through the water. The water was very muddy. Ananda was in a hurry because he had to get water for the Lord. He started trying to clear the water as best he could, but he couldn't do anything. He struggled, but he couldn't find any water that was drinkable. Finally, he ran back to Lord Buddha and said, "I'm so sorry. I couldn't get you water". Buddha asked, "What happened, Ananda? Why couldn't you get water? We saw a stream right over there, it's right over there". Ananda said, "I found the water but it was very muddy and when I tried to make it cleaner, I couldn't". Buddha said, "Ananda, now go back to that place and get me water". Ananda ran back to that place and found crystal clear water. All the dust, all the mud by then had naturally settled.

For most of us, what we try to do is from our ego. It is our vanity. We struggle to make life fit into the expectation, into the understanding, that has grown in us over years of practice. We always try to set things right our way. We are like Ananda, trying to get drinkable water by frantically stirring the water. We remain thirsty; we can't have water that is clean.

Thus, it often happens when negative comes to you that, if you try too hard to fix it, if you force the situation, things only get worse. You try to manage things and nothing you do helps. At that point the best thing is to distance yourself a little, to witness the whole situation with a deep sense of trust in the Divine design. Just let go, without muddling with it.

If you let go, if you give the outcome to God and trust, there is time. Let time settle it. Time is the healer. We need to accept the heavenly energy which is always available, which can take care of all our problems, provided we learn the art of letting go, provided we surrender our doubt, and give the outcome to God.

Trust and patience: they are very important to the day-to-day management of our life. Trust in Divine Providence. Trust in the Divine Mother. Trust in the wonderful intelligence of the Cosmic Process. Then have patience. If I want something to heal, I should allow some time.

Each attachment, every expectation, is a seed that you sow to reap future unhappiness. There is such beauty in this Divine design! At certain times, sometimes in short intervals, you will be given shock treatments to help you understand that it is not good to expect. The design is continuously operating. You keep expecting that there should be no problems. Eventually, though, you find that you start contemplating, "Should I expect anything at all? Shouldn't I just let go?"

After all, you are seeking happiness and peace. You are not seeking anything else. Whatever may be the activity, whatever may be the thought, you are seeking happiness and joy and peace, nothing else. You find expectations have been leading you to misery and unhappiness. The time comes that you take stock of the whole thing, even if you don't read books and don't attend meditation classes. That doesn't matter because you are in the meditation class of the universe. Mother Nature will teach you. She teaches me; she teaches everybody. We create miseries with our expectations. Eventually, we learn. It is only when we expect nothing, when we offer ourselves and all outcomes to God, that we are flooded with peace and joy.

# PRACTICE

Whenever you are moving from one activity to another, make it a practice to pause. First, be grateful for what you have just completed and everything you learned from it. Then offer all of your efforts, the results and outcomes, in what you are about to undertake to God. Open your heart and still your mind, if only for a few seconds, to receive the nameless energies of Divine grace, inspiration and guidance. You are just receiving now. You are creating space in your heart and mind for Divine energy and creativity to move ahead of you, to form and express the Divine intention through this upcoming activity. Release all the outcomes to God and begin. Observe how you receive the guidance and inspiration you need to respond to each moment as it unfolds.

# KEEPING COMPANY WITH THE POSITIVE

IT IS NATURAL to be fearful. It is more natural to conquer fear. In truth, by nature, you are fearless.

Positive thoughts, courage and confidence, and continuous affirmations that make your path to God and God-Realization easier, are your best friends. You need to keep company with them always. That is the Holy Company that is already within your heart. Avoid the unholy company of the negativity of your mind. If you are in the company of the Holy One, the positive One, you will glow. You will be happy. You will be graceful. You will be full of life. You will celebrate every moment because you are alive; you are no longer the living dead. You are alive moment to moment, in awareness.

Life, by design, is a continual process of self-discovery. The more harmonious we become in our living, the more we bridge the gap between our thoughts inside and the world outside. We become more alert and conscious. We don't easily surrender to negative thoughts, to negative brooding, or to any negative bombardment from outside. We watch and pause; then we move as a true friend of the spirit.

All beings on earth and in the myriad of universes are eternally connected to the Divine source. Each plant, each animal, each natural element, each human being, is a sublime manifestation of Divine life, an exquisite incarnation of Divine beauty and love, an embodiment of Divine nature. Study this in your heart and in your experience. The world around you is living revelation.

Your life and all life around you is the loving touch of the living body of God. Even the harshest and most fearsome manifestations of human life are sources of Divine revelation. They teach us, however painfully, of the terrible and deadly cost of forgetting that our true life is rooted in and devoted to the Divine.

The Divine is within. It is forever singing through the world around us. Our task is to awaken to it until we see it everywhere, until we hear and feel it in every moment: in every aspect of the creation we encounter and the life we are given. As sincere devotees of the spirit, we train the mind, we attune our heart to the Divine at play within and around us. We contemplate these truths until we feel the Divine singing through the world and our own being, always.

# PRACTICE

Practice becoming watchful and alert so you can come to understand when your mind is going in the wrong direction. At that point, catch yourself. You can say, "No, my child, this is not the right way. You are my best friend. How could you talk like this? You are talking like an enemy. No. You are my best friend".

Embrace your mind with all love, with all compassion. Then find a way to lead your mind with thoughts of higher vibration, with thoughts of higher light, with the wisdom of those sages and saints who have illumined the path of reality for you.

In moments of leisure, take yourself to some place of tranquility where nature surrounds you, where there are big open spaces or huge old trees that are full of energy. Take yourself to that kind of place, a quiet spot for reverie, and sit. Contemplate. Commune with nature. Commune with the birds. Commune with the leaves rising and falling with the wind. Commune with the movement of rippling water. Commune with the rhythms of the life around you. Open your body and mind to the rich, subtle harmonies of the natural world, the world that gave birth to you. Let those harmonies lead you deeper into the peaceful harmonies of your own spirit.

Redirecting your mind when it begins to fall into negativity and immersing yourself in the deep natural harmonies of your true being, you enlighten your mind. You begin to walk the path of your life in an enlightened state. Negative mechanisms and habits of mind will no longer be able to grip you. They will not be able to steer you off course because you have taken the helm of your own mind. Ultimately, nothing will be able to put you into fear, anxiety, stress, or strain.

# BLESS ALL, HARM NONE
# WITH YOUR WORDS

THE GIFT OF speech is so commonplace to human beings that we fail to appreciate the true magnitude of its power to bless or to harm. Words have incredible power. That power, how we can use it to bless others, how we misuse it to hurt others, and the thoughtless habits we fall into with regard to it, all offer us an immense resource for cultivating mindfulness.

We are all insensitive from time to time. There are times when we regret something we say. We lash out in anger. We gossip. We fall into teasing without realizing the personal cost to the one on the receiving end of our humor. We can be oblivious to the threshold at which a joke becomes ridicule. We need to take care, when we are speaking, that we are not doing so at the expense of any other human being.

In a group, we often derive enjoyment at the cost of others. We talk easily of others' faults and weaknesses, often simply because we don't know how else to keep a conversation going.

We find endless and myriad ways to put others down — in order to elevate ourselves in our own mind or in the minds of others — all without grasping the damage we are doing to ourselves and to those about whom we speak so harshly.

Without conscious awareness, words can be hurtful. We realize it too late, after the damage is done, when the words cannot be taken back. Then, any effort we make to correct our mistake often only makes it markedly worse.

We forget that our view is distorted. We cannot see anything as it is. We have a pathetically limited frame of reference. When we are judgmental, we are like a strainer trying to find fault with a hole. We search for the faults in others while overlooking our own imperfections.

Our judgmental thoughts and comments create difficult situations. At the very least, they send negative energies into the world that replicate their own virulent essence. Be mindful of any act that hurts others. One day we must pay for every harm we do.

When we repeat harmful acts, they gradually become second nature to us. Their negative, discordant energies accumulate in our hearts and minds. They store themselves in our bodies, creating discomfort and disease. They multiply the possibilities for our personal disgrace and for harm to come to us.

Kind and loving words can bridge all differences. They create the foundations of peace and harmony in all relationships.

There are those who are true gifts to humankind. Their words are charged with positive energies that uplift and strengthen the human heart and soul. We are instantly rejuvenated in their presence. If for some reason they have to criticize, they do so with empathy, using constructive, encouraging and compassionate words. The other person never feels put down.

Be a true healer. The world has enough venom. There is a plethora of negatively minded people in every society. Don't join the herd. Stand up boldly. Speak in harmony with the path of enlightenment. By respecting others, you respect yourself. By uplifting others, you uplift yourself.

Give by being a good listener as well. When you learn to listen to the other's point of view with a non-judgmental mind, you hear beyond words. You feel and see who is speaking behind the words. From that place, the appropriate words come naturally to soothe and heal the wounds of others.

When your mind is filled with love and compassion, your heart will overflow with the urge to bless and heal others. Then all who meet you will be blessed. The pure mind is a pure blessing for all humankind. Pure mind sees the Divine in everyone. It sees the purity and perfection in everything!

# PRACTICE

Take the vow to bless all and hurt none! Cultivate greater awareness of how you use language. Become attentive to the quality of your speaking. What does it reveal about who you are being in this moment? What does it contribute to others? Where is this conversation coming from, where is it leading, at an energetic level? If you find yourself engaged in a negative conversation, remember your commitment to bless rather than harm. If necessary, openly admit you feel uncomfortable with being so negative, and explore with the other person how you both can redirect the conversation. If you find yourself in an angry, accusatory exchange, simply admit that this is not constructive for anyone and take a break. Search your soul for the capacity to accept and understand. Don't come back to it until you can be compassionate and constructive, until you can bless the other person with what you have to say and hear their side of the issue.

# ARISE, AWAKE, ACCEPT: THE THREE A'S OF YOUR PRACTICE

IF YOU DO not arise into your spiritual inheritance, if you do not awaken to your own mind and lift it into the light of higher truth, if you do not accept all that life brings you as the gift of God that it is, no amount of prayer, meditation, or spiritual practice will make a difference. You may sit before God. You may pray and meditate. You may perform other spiritual practices, but you will remain asleep. "Arise! Awake! Accept!" are the three A's of spiritual practice. They are essential. Until you embrace them as central, you cannot be other than subject to the whims and vagaries of your untrained mind.

Work the soil of your own mind. The more you do so, the more confident you become in life and in your own mind. You move away from fear and doubt. If you leave your mind to its own upward and downward cycles, however, the downward cycles gradually dominate. Gravity overtakes you. You feel more and more defeated. Fear and doubt and guilt begin to grip you. They live like parasites in your body and mind, sucking your life away.

You sleep for six to eight hours. For the remainder of your day, you only think that you are awake. The typical waking state, however, does not even approach wakefulness. Most of us remain deeply asleep. We eat, we talk, we see and respond to the people, the circumstances and the world around us in the dull and dim awareness of habit. We live unconsciously, existing within the limits of what we believe we already know. We are somnambulists, sleepwalkers.

The greatest challenge any of us faces in life is to wake up, to awaken from the sleep of unawareness into the joy of mindful awareness. The practice of awakening to the deeper, truer, more expansive realities within each moment, and of making the wisdom of the Masters our own, is essential to being human. Magnificent, subtle and uplifting dimensions of existence lie beyond the physical, beyond our current levels of awareness, beyond our current assumptions and beliefs. They are the healing, unifying leavens of life, a leaven which lifts us and, through us, lifts the world. They provide the fertile ground from which more humane qualities surface and mature for our own happiness and for the happiness of others.

When we are asleep, walking in unawareness, we miss the essential Being within. We never come to know our true Self, the one who is constant, the one who experiences. We never come to know true, enduring joy. We never come to know life itself. We live superficially, caught up in the external, in the excitement or frustration of the moment. Any occasional happiness is inevitably followed by unhappiness. We miss life's promise, what could be, what is meant to be.

Awaken your consciousness. Arise to claim the magnitude of your true inheritance. Until you awaken, you are vegetating, confined to your personal struggles and concerns. A larger life awaits you. Life is expansive. Spirit is expansive. You are expansive in your nature.

As you awaken and arise in the higher, unifying life of your spirit, you accept. You accept everyone you meet as a spiritual being, like yourself. Confronting your own limitations with compassion, you become more appreciative of the problems and weaknesses of others. You stop focusing on the material faults and ignorance of others. Anger and resentment toward those who cause you pain diminishes. You no longer fight against anyone else as "the enemy". The pain of others affects you as much as your own. Your concern for the less privileged deepens. As your spirit grows in understanding, you no longer fight against what comes to you. You perceive the sustaining grace available to you in all experience. You learn to trust, to accept where life is leading you.

As you continue to practice wakefulness, you accept the truth that God's grace alone is all-powerful. You surrender ever more deeply to the love and protection of the Divine as the simple way to peace. This is the path of your heart. You are now ready to accept the glory of Divine love and light. Arise, Awake, and Accept until you reach your Home.

# PRACTICE

In the simple path of *bhakti*, of surrender and devotion, you are watchful and keen. By the sheer force of habit, when doubt comes, watch it as a fleeting thought and apply the antidote of your love and trust in the God within. Let your faith in God give you enough confidence to rule out all doubt. Fill yourself with devotion and love and that will take care of all that you need in life. Tell yourself, "You are safely in the hands of God. You are not alone anymore. You and your Beloved are together. No fear, no doubt can survive in the enlightened shrine of my heart". Repeat this practice time and time again, until those doubts which bring you so much restlessness, the ones that destroy your inner peace and your harmony with others, have stolen away in silence. This is the power of *bhakti*, the power of the love for God.

—— ⁐ ——

# THE PATH THROUGH
# YOUR HEART

WITHOUT DEVOTION AND love, no effort on your part will bear the fruit of freedom. You cannot find God without first reaching your heart. Until you come to that place of love, you have nothing. All of the Great Ones had to come to that Supreme Love, that unconditional love. Devotion and love are the essence, the essence of the spirit and of life itself.

It is in the heart that we feel for others and for those who are close to us. When we establish our ultimate relationship with God, we grow closer in that relationship through our daily prayers, worship, chanting and spiritual companionship. Our heart opens a little bit at a time. The movement is incredibly subtle.

We are like a child being carried by the mother from one room to the other. The child doesn't know the mother has lifted her when she was asleep to move her to bed, but the movement has taken place. In the path of *bhakti*, in the path of devotion, love, and surrender, you work to erase your ego and to present a clean slate to your Beloved.

It is not always easy to perceive, it is not always easy to understand, how God is moving us. Only the Divine Mother knows. The child does not know. The Divine Mother takes us from one place to the other, from one level of consciousness to the other, in a continual process, without our knowing it.

That is the reason we should never lose heart. Even if at times your mind is not settling down on God. If devotional tears are not rolling down your cheeks, if you are not falling at the Divine Feet, don't lose heart. Your perseverance is what God wants to see in you, not what you do. God wants to see your steadfastness. Are you are ready to persevere in spite of the fact that you have not experienced anything whatsoever? Is your movement, your wish, your love, subject to certain experiences? If it is subject to certain experiences, you are putting obstacles to the path of your devotion and realization.

You will have inspirational flickers from time to time. Experiences will come to tell you, "Yes, I am listening to you. I am watching you. I know, step by step, you are crawling toward me like a small child". That is what spiritual experiences are about. They encourage and inspire you to keep going through the arduous journey. They are not the journey itself, however; they are not the point of the journey.

Be childlike. With absolute innocence in your heart, offer yourself unconditionally to God. Surrender. Embrace the ways in which God moves you to higher ground through every experience, whatever it is. You don't need conditions. Everything that comes to you comes from God; it is the loving hand of God's personal instruction for you. Within every experience is a call to the Divine child in you to awaken. Make up your mind. Whether you have established your relationship with the Divine through the guru or directly, whichever suits you, move through complete surrender and trust.

What is important is your doubtless state of mind.

Love and doubt are conflicting conditions. They don't go together. Love and doubt are incompatible. If you doubt someone you love, they feel hurt. If you love God, if you say you love God, and in spite of that you nurture doubts, you love but you doubt. A love with doubt is self-contradictory. We must recognize this truth.

# PRACTICE

We notice when we are nurturing doubts. When doubts come, we watch them. We counteract doubt by thinking of it as a dark patch, a shadow enveloping the mind and heart. The only way to drive out darkness is with light. So we hold all sense of darkness, all shadow, all doubt tenderly in the light, opening our heart to the illumination that God will surely send.

If doubt is ever present, there is another side, which is trust. You have only to say to yourself, "Yes, I have doubt in my heart. So what! I also have tremendous trust in God. This doubt is nothing. This doubt cannot stay in my mind, because the power of my trust in my Beloved is so strong. The grace and light and strength of all the saints, all the masters, all the *Satgurus* are always available to me, always with me. Doubt cannot stay".

Know that all negativity, all doubt, is trivial and utterly powerless when you hold yourself in the light of all the Holy Ones, when you cling to the feet of your *Satguru*. Practice this. Resolutely meet all doubt by affirming the loving, reliable presence and grace of God and the Master in your life.

# THE WORLD: A PLACE OF LEARNING

THE SOUL AND consciousness evolve through experience. The world is a place of continuous learning. The mind carries its impressions forward, from one body to another, from one birth to another. This is the journey of life that does not stop with death. Death is only a short pause between two levels of experience, gross and subtle. You leave the gross body to enter into the subtle plane of consciousness. If your consciousness is governed by earthly desires, however, you must return again to the grosser level of the body to work through those desires. You keep coming back until you learn to perceive what is real and eternal and to let go of what is unreal and transient.

Living in the world, a world of continual change, it is only natural to become identified with the body and its senses. The magnitude and quantity of gross phenomena around you tends to overpower the more subtle aspects of consciousness. Inevitably, though, you come to experience certain difficult situations which function like natural shock treatments.

Whether you are illiterate or highly educated, rich or poor, you stumble over obstacles at times which appear insurmountable. You suffer.

There are times of annihilation, of utter devastation, in every life. No one escapes. These, too, are part of the human experience. If you learn how to respond to these obstacles, how to receive the deepest wounds of your humanity in a way that opens your heart and expands your consciousness, your spirit is revealed. You find healing. You are freed from the tyranny of circumstance. You are purified by the process.

That is what surrender is all about. If you humbly surrender, if you accept the wounds as well as the joys of life when they come, if you resolutely dive deep within to see with the eyes of the soul, wisdom is born. Compassion is born.

That is why Jesus taught, "Resist not evil". What we resist persists. We become like that which we love. We also become like that which we hate. Which will be stronger in you, your love, your compassion, your forgiveness, or your hate, your resistance?

Accept the blow of even the hardest teaching when it comes. Drive deep, deep within yourself to find that place from which you can derive peace and understanding and compassion with regard to what is happening to you. When you confront the internal or external carnage brought about by human ignorance, greed and hatred, take refuge in God, in the eternal principles. Surrender. Allow the soul to nourish you. Allow all that is not your essential being, all that is not your essential goodness, to be shaken loose in the storms of your life. Be the reed shaken in the wind for God's hidden purposes, even when they elude you. For "he who loses his life shall save it, and he who saves his life shall lose it".

The obstacles, the agonies of your life then become entrances into the world of spirit. They are initiations into *bhakti*, into deeper devotion and compassion.

Life will not be confined to your preconceptions of what it should be. It is infinite. It is exquisite in its subtlety. It is relentless in its workings to reveal its Oneness. Let the outer shell of your illusions be shattered, so that you are no longer an instrument of the illusion which is a scourge upon the earth. Whatever you are experiencing is ultimately beneficent if you choose to discover the beneficence. Then you become a co-creator with God, gleaning every aspect of the love God extends to you.

However much a disbeliever we might have been, most of us eventually come to believe that there is some greater power, some higher intelligence, some higher design at work. We get glimpses into other realms through our joys and sorrows. Those realities take root in the heart. Possessive, materialistic attitudes gradually lose hold. The energy level of the mind rises and we begin perceiving newly.

I met a wonderful old woman in Crestone, Colorado, one of the most highly charged spiritual places in the U.S.A. When I was talking to her, she said. "You know, I learned a lesson from this machine [from which she receives oxygen]." She lived at an altitude of 8,000 feet. She didn't need extra oxygen at 300 feet in St. Louis. She said, "This machine has taught me something. Always before in my life, I thought I breathed. Now, I know I have no power, not even to breathe".

The day you come to realize that you don't even have the power and freedom to breathe, that day you truly become a devotee. Not before. Before that, you are only moving toward becoming a devotee.

Devotion is a commitment. It comes only through deep experience. It can't be borrowed. It doesn't come from books. If it does come, it never leaves you. The feeling that she can't breathe never left the woman in Colorado until the day she died. As long as she understood that she didn't even have the freedom to breathe, she also knew the only thing she did have was faith. She told me, "Now I have faith in God. I don't understand much. I don't read much. I have no knowledge. But, yes, I have faith". What is faith, but love and trust in God?

We have love in our heart. That is natural. We give that love to anyone, to everything in the world, but we don't give it for its own sake. In return, we want happiness. We hope everyone we trust will return us a little happiness. In so doing, in so giving, we are disappointed. We suffer. Gradually, we learn. We finally come to see that what we were seeking was only our imagination, our expectation. It was not reality. Only then we seek the Ultimate Reality.

# PRACTICE

Practice inquiring of yourself, "What kind of true freedom do I enjoy? What pseudo-freedoms do I cling to? What kinds of bondage do I create for myself? How do I enslave myself with what I buy from the marketplace? How do I chain myself in the relationships with which I fill my time? What kinds of attachments fetter my body, mind, intelligence and spirit? Accept the pain of your attachments rather than judging them. Allow them to lead you to that place where you can say, "No, this is too painful. It is better that I cling only to God".

Practice surrendering to God as your true resource, your only source of wealth, your only security. Cling to God through the storms of your life. Rely on God for all the comfort, love, and assurance you have been seeking elsewhere. Let go of everything else but your trust in God.

# YOUR HEART AS THE CENTER OF THE UNIVERSE

TRUE DEVOTION, TRUE surrender, true trust in God comes experientially. It can't be given to you. Who will have this experience, the time at which they will have it, is known only to the One. Feel blessed that you were given a human body, a human mind, a life in which to grow and learn, a heart. Your heart is a center of the world, a center of the universe. Bring all of your experience, the whole of the universe, through your open heart. Hold the whole world in your heart. When your heart is open, you feel for everybody, for every being. Then your heart beats, not only with blood, but with the rhythm of the universe, with the rhythm of Divine ecstasy.

The more concentrated you become in your love, in opening to Divine light, in surrendering to the Divine will in everything you do, the more you become a Divine instrument. Release all that is gross and negative through prayer, submission and love. Sensitively attune yourself to the Divine, so the Divine can move through you without obstruction. Visualize all negative in you being burned away whenever it arises. Offer any suffering as an oblation into the fire of your heart. Your energy will begin to elevate. As you move to higher, subtler, and more sublime realms, you will find that the God you had thought far away from you is closest of all. God is in your heart. God resides there. Whenever you close your eyes to go to your inner shrine, you find that you and your Beloved are in a beautiful union of love and devotion.

In that center of love, you are wedded to your Beloved. When action flows out of you, when thoughts come, you find they are worship. They are no longer your actions and your thoughts. They are God's actions and God's thoughts, because you are opening yourself up for God to work through you.

Your world remains the same. Your relations, your kin, your friends, your work, remain the same. You change. You change and everything changes. You surrender yourself to the Divine in your own heart, knowing fully well that you are absolutely secure, eternally secure in the Divine lap. You are safely in the strong hands of Divine power and love and compassion.

## PRACTICE
Practice consciously bringing your experiences through your heart. To begin, select one situation which confounds,

perplexes or frustrates you. It could be one about which you have become resigned. Hold the entire matter prayerfully in your heart, as you talk intimately to God about it. Explore every aspect of the situation with God, your personal confidante. Ask all the questions you have. State all of your concerns, considerations, and misgivings. Ask for new light, new understanding, a new path leading you where you need to go with this aspect of your life. Continue coming back to God, as you hold the situation in your heart, until it is resolved. The love of God never fails. Devotion is ever blessed.

# WE ARE ALL SEEKERS OF
# *ANANDA:* JOY, BLISS ETERNAL

WE ALL ARE radiant spirits. We are all embodiments of bliss eternal — embodiments of pure, Divine love. As such, we are all seekers of *ananda*. The whole human community is an *ananda* community. We are all seeking happiness. We all are seeking the joy of our true being.

None of us wants to be afflicted with diseases and suffering. Yet, these are part of our daily life. The goal of our life is to realize that we are not this fragile body, this fragile mind, this fragile intelligence which changes, dies, and decays. We are that which was never born and that which shall never die.

We do not want to be unhappy in life because our true nature is happiness. None of us wants to die because we are deathless. The only purpose of the spiritual journey is to realize this. Everyone is afraid of the journey, nonetheless, because it treads a path unknown, uncharted, uncertain. It is unpredictable.

You have to give up your ego — who you think yourself to be — in order to experience your infinite reality. That is the biggest problem. We are afraid. We are afraid that if we give up our ego, we will be non-existent; but we are no more than vegetables until we awaken to complete, childlike trust in the Divine.

What is most precious to God is our complete trust. We are all meant to have a child's trust in our Beloved, to sing to God of our love and trust with absolute abandon. When, in innocent surrender and delight, we manifest complete trust in all our actions, in all our thoughts, in all our deeds, we have a child's trust. Our husbands and wives, our mothers and fathers, our children and co-workers, our neighbors and friends will feel that one reality in our heart and all will be blessed immeasurably.

# PRACTICE

MEDITATE ON ALL the gifts that God has given you. The most sublime gifts are your body and your mind. Contemplate the miracles that God unfolds through your body and mind, through the body of the world, at every moment. You cannot even breathe without God breathing through you. Fill with gratitude and your love for God for all that you have been given. You are heir to the entire universe. The kingdom of mind, which is your birth right, is union with your Divine Mother and Father and with all of Creation. Affirm to yourself time and again that you are the embodiment of *ananda*, joy eternal, that no speck of doubt or disease can touch your spirit. In spirit, you are eternally pure and peaceful. Chant *"Om Shanti, Om Shanti, Om Shantihi" in* the rising and falling rhythms of your breath.

# THE AVAILABILITY OF DIVINE GRACE

HUMAN CIVILIZATION HAS been on a long journey, evolving toward ever higher levels of consciousness. Throughout every age, God has sent the saints and sages to earth. They are living, breathing beacons of the destination of our own journey. They work eternally to uplift humanity and the human spirit. They hold our hands to guide us into the highest dimensions of life. Those dimensions are beyond the perception of the physical body and the physical senses. They are beyond this physical, manifested world.

The sum total of all the grace of the Enlightened Ones, of all their prayers and austerities, of all their spiritual practices, the sum total of all the blessings which have emanated from them, are emanating from them at this moment. Those vibrations, that grace, those blessings, are in the ether. The sublime vibrations of all those who have been living a holy life, the life dedicated to Divinity, are always around us. All of that Divine grace surrounds us. It permeates every atom of the universe, and is always available to each of us.

Grace is always working on a very subtle plane. Maybe many of us are not conscious of it, but it is working. It is working every time we have an intuitive glimpse; every time we have a subtler feeling; every time we are drawn into something good, toward something higher in life. Every time we have a glimpse of mercy or goodness; every time good comes to us from some unknown, unseen source; every time such things happen in our life, it is, again and again, Divine grace. It is the blessings of the Holy Ones who have worked for the betterment of human consciousness throughout time.

## PRACTICE

Take a moment to open your heart to the infinite Divine grace of the Holy Ones each morning. Affirm in your mind the truth that the Self-Realized Masters never die, that they merely give up their physical bodies to be eternally available to all of humankind, transcending time and space. Receive the tender and countless blessings they wish to bestow on you this day. Let the energy of those blessings fill you, body, mind, and soul. Then offer yourself as an instrument of those blessings to others. See and feel Divine love, Divine light, the incomprehensible blessings of the Holy Ones, pouring through your heart and out to all those you meet as you go through the day. Send those blessings out, to touch and uplift all other beings on earth, to heal all beings who are suffering. Become the radiant channel of blessings for all children of our Mother, the Earth.

# LEARNING TO SEE WITH THE EYES OF THE SPIRIT

EVERYTHING IN OUR lives is a part of the process of human evolution. Everything we do is for the whole of human society in its process of evolution to a higher state of consciousness. Our human experience compels us to question life, to question ourselves, more deeply. That is the design of the life process.

What are we seeking? What is the source of true happiness? Is it more things? Or, is it discovering the bliss, the *ananda*, of our essential being? What leads to true peace?

The questions bring new light to the human mind. We discover the need for a different perspective, the need to learn to see beyond the physical dimension, the need to see with the eyes of the spirit.

Those who have lived the eternal principles through the ages have left us a legacy, but it is one with which we need to personally experiment. We must find out whether these principles are practice-able in our own lives, in the day-to-day struggles of our own existence. It is only through practice that we experience truth directly. It is only through practice, through our own experience, that we truly learn.

We humans, according to all the Enlightened Ones, can never find peace until we pause. We must withdraw from our senses. Our senses are naturally focused externally. Our energies move outward to the manifested Cosmos, in continuous interaction with the world. That outward focus of sensual pursuits creates a constant energy drain.

When we rise up, when we bring those energies together to focus them inward in a contemplative, meditative endeavor, we discover a new, untouched dimension. We discover the wealth and treasure that lies in the Holy of Holies, in the inner shrine that is our heart. There God sits, the eternal Presence.

God is not sitting in silence in our hearts. God sings a song of eternal joy. In India, we call it the Song Celestial, the *Bhagavad Gita*. The Lord is not mute. He is sitting with a flute. He is calling us. He is calling us all into that world of joy, which is the shrine of our heart, the essence of our being, our own self.

Though we seek and search outside, depending on external things to find happiness, we find true happiness only through our longing and deepening desire to move within. There we experience the Celestial Song Divine, the *Gita*, not as a concept, but a sweet, living reality.

# PRACTICE

Practice responding to the faintest stirrings of your own heart. They are the quickening of your soul. They are the delicate and vulnerable stirrings of the new life which seeks to be born through you. Practice noticing them, listening to them, spending some time with them.

Retreat inward when something stirs you. If necessary, go back to it during your evening *sadhana*. Explore those feelings, those moments of inspiration of your heart quietly, a little more fully, each day. Journal about them. Let them gather in your mind and heart. Let them lead you to your deepest aspirations and longings. Let them move and flow and work through you until they become intimate friends, until they literally sing and their singing fills every cell of your body. That, too, is prayer.

These are the threads of your unfolding. Given your full, absorbent attention, they will gather in the eyes of your soul like the faint light of distant stars, until they can be seen and understood, until they can find ways to fully express themselves through you.

# ON DESTINY, INDIVIDUAL WILL, FREEDOM AND GRACE

AROUND THE WORLD, seekers of different faiths and traditions ask if our lives are predestined. The simple and truthful answer is yes. The past has created the present. The present creates the future. Destiny continues to unfold as a matter of cause and effect. What is, both in our own lives and in the life of the world around us, is proceeding from what has been.

The answer, however true, gives rise to an even more important question. If everything is predestined, what is the role of individual will? Do we have any freedom? This is a difficult, confounding, enduring mystery for humankind.

As long as we are ignorant of our true identity, as long as we have not found our inner existence, our Eternal Reality, our lives are predestined. Only by finding the authentic being, the true Self within, which is infinite existence, knowledge and joy, can we unravel the mystery of destiny.

We cannot borrow the answer. No philosophy can resolve this ancient riddle of human existence. The essential question, the one that must be personally answered, remains: Who am I?

The self you think yourself to be, the self with whom you have been identified, is limited. It is a pseudo-self, a limited self that is governed by the past. It is the ego, the obstacle between you and the realization of a more ultimate freedom. As long as you are in the grip of the ego's narrow illusions, you cannot be free. You are a prisoner of the past and the destiny that proceeds from it.

It is only by mastering your own mind that you escape the inevitable wheel of destiny and the confines of individuality. If you are circumscribed by individuality, you are within its operational range, whether you accept it or rail against it. Enlightenment is the transcendence of individuality through universality. Being one with the One, the Enlightened Masters have nothing to do with destiny or individuality.

The only way to transcend the ego is to become conscious, to continually surrender your limited awareness into an ever expanding awareness of the Universal Oneness, to rely ever more deeply on Divine grace.

Grace is important. We all have individual will power. Everything that we have achieved in life has come out of our intention and will to attain. We all have the aspect of effort, our individual will to attain. Our effort combines with the grace of the Divine, which unfolds to assist us in achieving our goals. Without Divine grace, nothing can be achieved.

With grace, all that is impossible becomes possible. All of life's obstacles become steps toward higher realization. We open our hearts to Divine grace and grace opens our heart to realize the purpose of every situation presented to us. Until and unless we open to grace, we cannot transform the more difficult situations of our lives. With grace, even the most negative forces become agents for the positive, lifting us into a higher life, into higher energy, into more expansive consciousness.

Our hearts must open in acknowledgment of the Divine grace that surrounds us. It is not enough to read scripture and participate in spiritual discussions. More important is to practice opening to Divine grace, to let grace sing in our lives, until we realize the Celestial Song is the song of our own heart.

# PRACTICE

As you end your morning meditation each day, spend a few moments consciously holding your heart open to the grace that God is bestowing on you and the coming day's activities. If you find yourself in a difficult situation during the day, turn inward again, to the presence of grace. Feel the energy of grace flowing through you, into the situation, into the hearts of any others involved. If you have a saint or guru to whom you have special devotion, call on that intervening, grace-filled presence. Let grace inform and guide you as to how to respond to the situation. What conduct, what attitudes, what changes, what courses of action on your part, would be in alignment with grace? Surrender the smaller, lower, more predictable impulses of the ego and follow through with a path informed by grace. Cultivate awareness of and offer gratitude for the magnitude and availability of grace, and the difference it makes, in the quality of your daily life.

# BECOME A YOGI!

Who is a *yogi*? The *yogi* is one who understands the limitations of individuality, the falsehood of the personality. The *yogi* is one who understands the falseness of appearances and tries to penetrate reality. The *yogi* is one whose heart is longing to be in union with the Cosmos. The *yogi's* heart melts at the suffering of others. The *yogi's* heart, the *yogi's* mind, is not clinging to selfish interests.

The *yogi* is one who is contemplative, who is meditative. The *yogi* is one who cultivates a positive, befriending mind, the continual, living awareness of the full truth of his or her existence. Through meditation, the *yogi* realizes what a great gift it is to be a human being.

What a great gift it is to have a human mind! What a grace to have this wonderful, unique system of mind, heart and soul, which can commune with Nature in totality, provided we keep the instrument properly tuned.

Regular practice is essential. Everyday practice. Practice. Practice. Practice. Practice being more awakened. Practice being more aware. Practice being more accepting. Practice becoming more conscious. Practice understanding the presentations of life that come to you. They come to you at every moment from an unknown, unseen Divine source.

The more we are open to this reality, the more we can listen to that Song Celestial which is going on in the heart of our hearts, we don't only remember God when we are in distress. Then we remember God, we remember grace, we remember the love which surrounds us, at every moment. We recognize light. We recognize its source: the Light of all lights that is God. We don't forget that for a moment. We realize that we don't see through our eyes. We know that God sees. God sees through our eyes. God is the doer.

Then we know: the source is universal. The source is Divine. My eyes can see only through the light of the Divine. My ears can hear only through the light of the Divine. My heart can beat only through the light of the Divine. My whole being pulsates and lives only through the being of the Divine.

The more you feel Divine grace within every moment, the more you open yourself to it, acknowledging it in your prayers, in your words, in song, in chanting, in mantras — in all your practice — the more Divine grace grooms your mind.

Divine grace disciplines your mind, trains your mind, soaks your mind with Divine love. One day, your mind will melt. Your ego will melt. Your ego then becomes supple, humble, simple. The more the ego becomes humble and supple, the more wisdom dawns in you.

It is the ego, our sense of separation, which is the obstacle to wisdom and to all that is our essence. The more we remove our ego from the path, the more we allow Divine light to penetrate through us, the more we begin to recognize everything happening around us as the moving hand of grace.

What is needed is to practice cultivating the befriending mind. We need to befriend ourselves by discovering our one, true friend. What is needed is to practice *yoga*, to practice union. To practice *yoga* is to be humble. It is to be simple. It is to be available to others, to be available to the highest energies of the universe, to allow them to flow through us for the good of the world.

All the *yogis* of the world have said it time and again: Nothing can be achieved until and unless you open your heart and surrender yourself to the higher power of the Divine. Nothing can be healed until and unless you acknowledge the magnitude of your own limitations and seek that Divine power, that Divine love, that Divine compassion which is infinite and limitless. Nothing can change for us until and unless we reckon with the limitations of individuality by which each of us is separated from the Indivisible Cosmic Principle. Until and unless we recognize that it is this separation from the Cosmos, this separation from the whole of Cosmic Consciousness that is the root of all our miseries, there is no escape from suffering.

Ignorance creates all separation. Until and unless we pierce our ignorance of the nature of individuality, we remain shrouded, clouded, and imprisoned by a mind that identifies with this tiny body. That is the bottom line of all the agonies of our lives! Until and unless we understand this deeply, true longing for a spiritual awakening cannot happen.

Meditation can happen only when we open our heart to this reality, to this dimension. As long as we are sensually bound, as long as we are emotionally bound, we are fettered. Until and unless we try to open ourselves up to that Divine light, Divine grace cannot flow through us.

We are the ones creating the obstructions and obstacles. We are the ones who suffer. We have created our own miseries. We are also the ones who can create happiness for ourselves.

There is the need for a fundamental acceptance. We cannot make anyone or any situation responsible for our unhappiness in life. We need to bring all the focus to our individual self to find out what the larger, infinite Self is all about. Then we come home to the realm of our own mind.

It is in the mind that we are bound. It is in the mind where we can be totally freed. It is in the mind where we feel bondage and pain. It is in the mind, also, where we can feel bliss, the joy of true freedom.

We can experience true freedom provided we are not shackled, provided we don't cling to petty desires. If we open ourselves, if we acknowledge that this human birth, this human body, this whole human existence has a deeper purpose to uncover, we find the path to freedom. The more we remind ourselves of that deeper purpose, the more we become an instrument moving toward Unity.

Every time I do good, all goodness dawns in me, all goodness comes into me. That is the message of the positive, befriending mind. It is the message of the *Gita*. It is the message of *yoga*. It is a simple message of awakening.

We all are born to awaken. We are born to awaken from the slumber of our unconsciousness, to awaken from our ignorance which is the root cause of all unhappiness. We are all born to fulfill our own nature and our nature is Divine. Grace is eternally available to all of us. No small effort toward awakening goes in vain. Brick after brick, each step takes us toward the mansion of our true, Divine home.

May the Divine grace of God touch all our hearts. May it open our heart's center and the music that is the *anahat naad*, the unstuck sound of silence, the music that flows only from the Divine, Eternal, Cosmic Self. May we grow out of all our worldliness, narrowness, limitedness, into the world of unlimited, infinite Divine grace, joy, love and compassion.

# PRACTICE

God is within us, our one, true Beloved. Spend some time in silence each day with your Beloved. Find a quiet, peaceful place. Sit comfortably erect. Relax your body from head to foot, focusing on relaxing each body part. Then take a few deep breaths. Inhale deeply and exhale deeply, being conscious that you are breathing in and out. This is the first step of withdrawal from external perceptions. Now bring your mind to your nostrils and watch the flow of universal energy, *prana*, moving in and out. You are consciously connected with the *vishwa-prana*, the universal life force that sustains all life. This is spontaneous *pranayama*. Feel the beautiful rhythm of your life currents through the breath.

Thoughts will come and go to take you away from your concentration. Don't worry. Don't condemn your thoughts. Don't condemn yourself. Just relax. Bring your focus back to your breath and keep breathing. Keep watching your breath mindfully. Let your thoughts go into the rising and falling of the breath. You will now experience lightness in your body, calmness of you mind, and peace in your heart. Pray to God for Divine love alone.

Come out of meditation gradually, bringing your mind to the body. Thank God for the gift of your wonderful body and mind. Relax, bring your consciousness to the external world and feel all is well in your life. Bless everything around you when you open your eyes. Celebrate and be joyful for this gift of meditation and your union with love Divine.

# THE WAY TO GOD IS THROUGH YOUR OWN NATURE

It is necessary that the seeker of truth contemplate on the Self. You must discover your own nature. Human beings travel through different *gunas* of the mind, from the lower *tamasic,* to the higher *rajasic,* to the highest illumination of the *sattwic.* There is nothing to judge. It is simply a matter who is in what part of the process, in the various arenas of life. Depending upon the individual's nature, one treads the path toward final unity.

Are you a *sattwic* person, a *rajasic* person, a *tamasic* person, or a combination of all three? What is the pull of your own nature? To study one's own nature at close proximity makes the path easier. If you are a person who is a *rajasic* type, you have a very active mind. You have a lot of ambitions, a lot of things to achieve, a lot of things to do, a lot of unfulfilled desires cramming your mind. You feel they are your first priority. You have to do, do, do. You have so many things to do. There is a lot of force, a lot of activity involved.

For such an active mind, the path of *karma yoga* is best, because such a person is very dynamic. For such a dynamic person, a *sattwic* path of pure meditation, of sitting in one place in contemplation for long periods of time, would be difficult. It would be forced. *Karma yoga* is more natural. Then everything is done with dynamism, with enthusiasm, while searching the true Doer of all actions.

One who is *rajasic* in nature only has to become more alert; more conscious in performing the actions of the day-to-day; more and more conscious of the Doer within, the God within and the God without. The devotee closely observes and asks: Are these actions driven by the desires of my ego? Are they sincere offerings of my heart to please and serve the Divine? Are they motivated by selfish concerns or by selfless dedication? What is the force behind my motivation?

God only looks to the motivation of what we do and what we think. It is not what I am doing that is important. It is my attitude, my motivation, the energy of my being that becomes important.

Even mundane activities of a *rajasic* person gradually become focused on the Divine Doer as the devotee becomes more focused, conscious, and aware of the Divine potential within. The Divine is ultimately the source of all thoughts, the source of all actions, the source of all energies, the source of consciousness. The more we become aware of this, the more we grow on the path of spirituality.

A person who has grown beyond this active, hectic, dynamic life, who has seen enough of it and who doesn't find any charm in it anymore, has graduated. For that devotee, who is *sattwic,* the pull is toward a more contemplative, simple, humble life of surrender. Push that devotee into activity and he or she will not show much interest. It is not his or her nature — and the way to God is through our own nature.

Mind you, there is a very subtle difference between a *sattwic* person and a *tamasic* person, though they may look alike. A *tamasic* person will always try to avoid work. He or she will try to avoid activity and escape responsibilities. More surrendered to the demonic forces, a *tamasic* person is unstable, docile and passive.

A person who is *sattwic* might appear to be a person who is not interested in an active, ambitious life, but that person is of a stable and harmonious mind. He or she understands reality more deeply than a *rajasic* or *tamasic* person.

A *sattwic* person always chooses *sattwic* food, *sattwic* literature, *sattwic* company, endeavors and surroundings that promote unity with the Divine. The *sattwic* person gravitates toward anything that helps to unfold the Divine rather than the ego. With the ego, the *sattwic* devotee always tries to move ahead, to free himself or herself from its dominating clutches. The *sattwic* person is more surrendered to the Divine will, more surrendered to Divine love. He or she accepts life in its totality, without resistance, without judgment, without reaction.

Yes, you can generalize. There appear to be two doors through which to enter the Kingdom of God. One is through the head, through reason. The other is through the heart, through emotion. Though you may initially choose one due to your own nature, you inevitably must walk through the other. If you move through the heart, you come to realize the essence of wisdom. If you move through the head, the time comes when your wisdom is soaked in Divine love and ecstasy. They are intermingled. They cannot be isolated one from the other.

The path of discrimination, an analytical inner search for the Self, is always good. It is founded upon sound inner research.

Devotion will gradually refine your emotions. Emotions are unbridled when contaminated with material identification. As long as emotions cling to human beings or material objects, their focus is on the external. Such emotions drain you. They come back to you tainted, with blemishes. They cannot give you pure bliss, pure happiness. Though you may love, it is love for something in the world, something by its nature impermanent and imperfect. You can never attain peace through it. That is the nature of emotion given to anything impermanent.

The same emotion, the same love, the same heart opened to the Divine in all beings, will gradually be refined. Gradually this will become Divine love. With Divine love, you do everything for your Beloved. It is as if you are breathing for your Beloved. It is as if you are seeing for your Beloved. It is as if you are singing, you are listening, you are doing everything for the sake of your Beloved. Your love then continuously intoxicates you from within. It permeates everything that is external to you. Whoever comes in touch with you feels the touch of your Divine love, without selfish motivation, without any sense of expectation or judgment. Love flows through you. It comes back to you manifold, because the more you love, the more you are filled with love. The more you love the Divine, the more the Divine loves you, the more you are filled.

Thus, constant self-analysis — a very keen and neutral self-analysis about where your ego is dominating, where you are drawn to impermanence, where you seek happiness outside of your own being, where you are drawn unconsciously — is invaluable. If you are alert to discriminate and understand this play of your mind, then you are awakened in the path of *jnana*.

Simultaneously, if your heart, your emotions and your love are open to the Divine, to Divine will and grace, if you are seeking and searching and touching everything with that Divine, then gradually your emotions brighten. There is a wonderful blending of the head and the heart which you become. Then your head is not imbalanced. Your heart is not imbalanced. Your head and heart are in harmony with each other. Your spirit lives in joy.

The spirit is freed from the cage of the mind and distorted emotions. Now the spirit is freed from all of its intellectual fantasies and is given totally, utterly, unconditionally to the Divine. Then, that which is eternally yours happens. You come closest to yourself. That is exactly what self-realization is.

You realize that you are not separate from your Beloved. You are not separate from your true Self. You and your Beloved are one. That is the purpose of human birth.

For householders, renunciates, monks and nuns, for all humans, the path is through the head, through the heart, to the Divine.

# PRACTICE

A great Himalayan Yogi who lived for 160 years gave a wonderful practice in order to know what kind of nature you truly have:

At night when you retire to bed, when everything is calm and you have done your day's job, instead of just falling into bed and going to sleep, sit down on the bed. In a deep mode of contemplation and surrender to the Divine, let your mind go. There are no external disturbances. You can focus on your mind and see where it goes of its own accord. What thoughts and images arise? Try not to judge. Let go. Let the mind go. Let it fly. Let it move where it will.

You will experience the mind coming to certain points again and again and again. You will see that there are certain dominant processes in the mind.

Repeat this exercise the next day also. Repeat it often when you are going to bed. Practice this. Let go of the mind. Allow it to float in a way that you observe it, without judgment, to see where it is ultimately going. You can discover what types of thoughts, what kinds of preoccupations, your mind is gravitating toward. That is the pull of your nature.

# OBSERVING YOUR MIND WITHOUT JUDGMENT

To MONITOR YOUR mind and thoughts, it is important to be neutral, to observe your thoughts without categorizing them. When you put things into categories of good or bad, you are being judgmental. Anything you identify as bad only becomes more powerful. We see that clearly in children. When you ask a child not to do something, it becomes almost irresistible to the child.

Your mind is nothing more than a child's mind. It resists any restrictions, any imposition from outside, because it loves freedom. It has been given freedom. A sudden withdrawal of freedom is never accepted or appreciated. The less judgmental you are to your mind, the less condemning you are, the less resistance you have, the better your mind will perform, the more cooperative and harmonious it will be.

Most people battle with the mind in meditation and in their daily work. They find what is wrong with themselves, how many mistakes they have made. They keep a running list. Then the pattern extends to others. Anything that brings about self-condemnation is not a spiritual path. While it is good and helpful to recognize mistakes, repeating that I have made this or that mistake doesn't send our mistakes away. Those who repeat a mantra of "sin, sin, and more sin" get caught in the morass of sin.

Be more watchful, more vigilant of your mind at play. What kinds of thoughts are coming to your mind? Be compassionate. Be understanding toward yourself. If you don't love yourself, you can't love God. You certainly can't love others.

The love of God happens only through love of Self. Any extreme self-criticism leads to suffering, to depression. Then you don't achieve much. Years roll by. You have been on the path of spirituality. You have been practicing this. You have been practicing that. You have been doing this *yoga*, that *yoga*, this meditation, that technique, but substantially, not much happens.

A *yogi* is in an unconditioned state. All others are in a conditioned state. A *yogi* is one who is no longer under the compulsion of any conditions. A *yogi* is one who never discriminates. His or her mind is free of conditions. The common person would discriminate between the water of the drain and the water of the Ganges, because his or her mind has been preconditioned that this is drain water, nasty. This is Ganges water, holy. These are conditions of mind. In a pure state of mind, these conditions no longer linger. To the saint, it is all God; it is all holy.

For an ordinary conditioned soul, we have our definitions. We have our categories. We have our priorities. We have preferences. We have our own concepts, our thoughts. As we move higher and higher, these conditions gradually dissolve. As these conditions dissolve and as you become more and more unconditioned, you find that your devotion, your love, your surrender are becoming purer and purer.

Conditions are the impurities of the mind. The guru gives a tremendous gift to the disciple. He deconditions the child, the disciple. He creates situations by which the disciple is gradually forced to surrender the conditions. The concepts and preferences that were so dear lose their grip. The disciple finds that they mean nothing to him. What comes to have true meaning is the will of the guru, the will of God.

The devotee starts surrendering the conditions, the preconceived notions, the programs of the mind, at the altar of the guru. One after the other, like oblations in the fire, the devotee offers them. With regular practice of this inner fire ritual, the mind is freed and purged of its impurities. All prayers and spiritual practices are basically to purify the mind, to decondition the mind, to empty the mind, so that the mind can be filled up by Divine grace, Divine grace, Divine grace. Then the mind becomes the Divine Mind, the Cosmic Mind, the Universal Mind.

In the Universal Mind, there is no pain, there is no pleasure. There is no insult and there is no praise. There is no play of opposites. In the Universal Mind, nothing of that can play any more. It is only in the individual mind that all these habits can play.

Unconditioned mind is universal. Once we have reached the state of unconditioned mind, it is like *samadhi*, the state of conscious, ecstatic union with the Divine. You are merging with the Infinite Divine, with the guru, with God.

# PRACTICE

Practice being non-judgmental, non-reactive, non-resistant. First, see what is happening to your mind. What are the thoughts that are coming into your mind? Watch your thoughts in a very compassionate meditation. You are separate from the thoughts. If you watch the thoughts and keenly observe them, you find each and every thought rising up, appearing for some time, then dissolving in no time, because you are not participating. You are not engaging your thoughts with condemnation or appreciation. Condemnation or appreciation is nothing but your energy being given to that thought. The energy of response forms and reinforces a memory in your mind. The memories then block the mind. If you witness without judgment, the thought comes and it dissolves. It cannot impress itself on you. It came, because it was a part of you. It stayed, because it had to stay for some time. Its impression was not strong because it could not find cooperation from you. It received no reinforcing energy, so it fell on its face.

If we keep watching our mind, we eventually become mindful that it is the mind observing the mind, without any judgment.

After you gain some skill in this, gradually, begin to follow your thoughts. From where is this thought arising and evolving? Where is it dissolving? From where does it come and where does it disappear? This second stage follows the thought trails.

Eventually, automatically, even the thoughts that were coming at random will be less and less in number. You become focused on the thoughts, without any judgment. As you find where each thought is coming from, as you find where it lingers and where it disappears, you discover you have begun to flow with the thoughts. Now it is as if you are a surfer. You are surfing the webs of the mind.

Previously, you fought with the water, with the waves. You could not surf. You were crashing into the water, falling and being shoved to shore. Now, you know how to surf the waves. You are no longer fighting, no longer resisting. You are moving with the waves. You have separated yourself a little.

Ultimately, you find that you can even catch the gaps between thoughts. Normally, we cannot catch them. We are not aware of our thoughts. The more conscious we become about our thoughts, the more conscious we become of our mind. This consciousness of our thoughts gradually brings to us a calmer mind, because our mind is not random anymore.

Anything you observe keenly calms down. Give your full attention to your hand or leg, or to a pain. After you observe for some time, it becomes quiet. This is the nature of consciousness and of unconsciousness. Anything you do unconsciously persists as long as you are unconscious. The moment you observe it and become conscious about it, it stops. Try this, try this in your life for some time, without categorizing, without judging.

You don't judge because thoughts are thoughts. Good and bad are definitions of your conditioned mind. You are already suffering from this condition of the mind. All of your suffering is from the condition of the mind.

# A WORD OF REASSURANCE

IF YOU ARE practicing, there are going to be moments, there are going to be times, when you are forgetful. That, too, is part of the process. The pain of forgetfulness is also a part of your experience. It impresses itself on your mind. Gradually, you come to truly realize that your self-forgetfulness, the forgetfulness of your Divine connection, is the reason for all your unhappiness. Otherwise, you really would never long deeply for a Divine connection.

All experiences of our day to day life, bitter or sweet, help us to realize that the ultimate solution comes only through spiritual longing. Solutions materialize provided we practice every day and remind ourselves, time and again. It is only through practice that we can realize the goal of our life.

What I would share with you is this: Intensify your practice. Take refuge in the Divine Name. Chant that Holy Name which is sweetest to your heart. Chant it more and more within you, in spite of the fact that you are restless in your mind. Don't worry about it.

It is understandable that you worry about mundane matters, but do not start worrying about your worship, your chanting, your prayers!

Be more loving of yourself rather than condemning and finding fault with yourself. Rejoice in the little that you can do in spirituality. Feel happy that, yes, God has come into your life. There are moments of forgetfulness. So what? God is with you. The more you appreciate yourself, the more you will feel the blessings of the Divine.

The positive is very much within you. The moment you begin to glimpse the positive within you, it grows. It grows with your nurturing attention. You will come to feel that you are flooded with Divine grace. Before that, you feel deprived. Before that, you feel that nothing is happening.

Nonetheless, everything is contributing to your awakening to your oneness with God. All the failures, all the negativity, all the tears — they are all contributing to that final state of awakening.

So accept that positive aspect of the process. Always refocus on the positive aspect of it. Rephrase the wording of your thoughts to build your strength and confidence. I have found this practice to bring tremendous benefit to the devotees I have taught. Develop the positive energy within you.

Repeat positive words in your mind. Speak positive words to the world and to your surroundings.

Surround yourself with beauty. Take time to be grateful for everything good that comes to you. You will grow in spiritual consciousness. You will feel, more and more, Divine energy coming to greet you. You will grow in confidence in this spiritual world.

# PRACTICE

Brush away the negative emotions, the negative patterns and ruts you find yourself in. They are like parasites trying to live on your own energy. Imagine them as trivial, small insects crawling on your shoulder. That is what they are. They are nothing in comparison to who you are in God, to the power of your spirit, to the measure of the grace God and the Holy Ones are extending to you. You are One with God.

Remind yourself of that again and again. No matter where you find yourself, simply begin again. Brush the insect of the negative away, time and again, as the nuisance it is. Then focus on the real, positive vibrations of your mind. God is within you. You have infinite light and Divine grace available to you.

Gradually you will grow out of all conflicts and confusion. The muddle has not come one fine morning. There is a cause to this effect. There have been such thoughts and practices for many, many years in the past. Accept that human reality. But if you are determined today to change it, if you practice every day to change it, you are assured by all the sages, by all the Enlightened Ones, that yes, by practice, you can alter this. You can reverse the process. If your practice was emotionally negative then, yes, your determination to be positive can take you back to the positive within you.

# GOD ASKS ONLY TWO CENTS IN RETURN FOR GRACE

GOD WANTS TWO cents from us in exchange for peace in life. *Dakshina* is the offering to the Divine, to the guru, the teacher of the soul. The guru wants just two cents from all of us. The first cent is trust — trust in the words of the master, in the teachings of the masters. *Shraddha*, in Sanskrit, means trust and faith. If the Enlightened Masters teach that through compassion you reach higher compassion, then you need to practice compassion. You need to practice forgiveness in your life. The more you practice it, the more you realize it. So the first thing that is very important is faith and trust. That is the first offering to the Divine that you need to give.

The second cent that we need to always offer to the Divine is our patience and perseverance. Patience in the material world pays. Patience in the spiritual world pays infinitely.

If we are not patient and persevering through all the tests and tribulations in our life, which are but blessings to us, we will not be able to reach a higher state. The greater the tribulations we face, the greater the potential for grace. We need to be prepared. We prepare by attuning our mind with trust and patience. Trust and patience are most important.

In family life, if you have trust between husband and wife, there is better harmony and balance. If you have trust between the mother and the children, there is better harmony and balance. If there is trust between superiors and junior staff, there is more harmony and peace. If you practice patience and perseverance, it can bring all the blessings of the Divine to you. With trust, with faith in all that God has presented to you in your life, offer your love and patience and perseverance, your steadfast devotion to God. Then move steadily forward, in harmony and balance.

## PRACTICE

Compassionately and relentlessly recognize the areas of darkness in your life. Trust that they have value in your life. Affirm that they too come from God. They are leading you to some awakening. They are invaluable teachers which enlarge your compassion and understanding. Call on the Divine light, along with your patient, persistent energy and prayerful effort, to enlighten them. The simple path of your spirit will open.

Spend time outside often, meditating on the beauty of the natural world and its harmonies. Allow those harmonies to enter you. Feel them as your own. Their nature is in you. Know that you are connected to the inexhaustible source of the Cosmos in your own heart. Gradually, all external forms come home to the one thread running through the garland of life.

Prayer, meditation and natural beauty will bless you with the growing awareness and experience of Oneness and peace.

# SERVING THOSE WHO SUFFER IS SERVING GOD

WHATEVER OUR EFFORTS to uplift others, we do only a little. What we receive is huge, incomprehensible. We do not do a lot. We receive a lot.

Those who visit our street schools on the footpaths of Kolkata, India, say the same thing. The children we serve are homeless. These children were born on the streets. They grew up on the streets. Their life is on the streets. When you meet them, when you talk to them, when you play with them, the language that they share with you through their hearts will become your deepest memory of India. These children will be imprinted in your mind. You will have seen a new **dimension**. You have seen God in a human face. You have met God in another human heart, and you are forever changed.

There can be beauty and joy in the midst of poverty. There are many agonies in the midst of affluence. I have seen this time and again in my life working with street children in India and during my travels around the world, among rich and successful people.

We come to know life more closely if we visit works of deep compassion. Our heart expands and, in the expansion, our spirit blooms. The ego melts. We come to see the importance and the joy of being a direct instrument, of doing what little we can do for others.

Whatever helps us to expand moves us into a deeper experience of life. Contraction pushes us into misery. Contraction is the soil for all the agonies of our life. Direct works of loving compassion are a platform from which you work to free yourself from bondage, from all attachments, by growing in love. You expand in compassion. Smallness falls away.

What is compassion? Compassion is the melting heart of the Master, the melting heart of the Divine Mother in service to Her children. When you experience compassion in your heart, or in the heart of another, know that it is the Master's heart, it is God's heart, melting in the human heart. You allow God to melt in your heart so that Divine compassion can flow through you to touch every other soul.

There is never a question of personal credit or discredit in true service. You have become the vehicle through which God's compassion, God's love, God's life is expressing itself.

It is your Master's power that manifests through your heart. You are a surrendered soul — a small, tiny little child in His or Her hands. You have no worries. You cry when you are hungry. You desire, demand whatever you want. She is there, the Mother, always providing. Why worry? Once you learn the art of trusting and surrendering to the Master, your burdens become increasingly light. You discover that what was difficult to achieve through your own effort becomes easy whenever you do your best and entrust the rest to the Divine.

Ultimately, the role of all world religions, the role of all spiritual practice, is to support us in becoming good human beings. First and foremost, we need to become good human beings, people who uncover and express the goodness of our hearts. That is essential. It is what spiritual practice is about.

# PRACTICE

Find a new way to contribute to another human being each day, to practice generosity of mind and heart. Notice how that expands your experience of the goodness and beauty of life, how that carries the feeling and spirit of your day forward. Extend the practice of compassion in your spiritual life beyond your immediate circle of self, friends and family. Find new venues of compassion through which to express your love for God by serving the living God in those who suffer.

# BLESSING FOR YOUR JOURNEY FROM DEATH TO IMMORTALITY

THERE IS A special manifestation when you have truly surrendered to God. You are at ease. There is no dis-ease. You are at ease with yourself. Yes, disease will come to the body. Disease will go from the body. You are at ease. Yes, death will come to the body. There is no disturbance, whatever comes. You remain untouched, unscathed, like the sky.

Such a life we can say is a Divine life. It has been moving with steady devotion from the lower to the higher, from ignorance to the ultimate wisdom of enlightenment. From fear of death, it has been moving with ever deepening trust in the Divine toward deathlessness and union.

May all the Enlightened Masters belonging to all faiths and traditions, whose Presence is eternal in the space in which we all live and breathe, bless us, so that we can realize the unbound, unlimited expansion of the spirit. May their grace touch and open the lotus within our hearts. When our heart is closed, we are worldly. We have the cataract of *Maya* on our eyes. May their grace touch the lotus within our heart. May they open the petals of the heart, one after the other, so we can manifest our potential of Divine love for the whole universe through our befriending mind.

May our love expand to touch and envelope all hearts, all beings. May we realize that we are not this tiny little dot of an ego existence, this shadow. May we know that we are One. That is the reality that the sages of India announce so authoritatively, so boldly with the words: You are without birth and without death. You are THAT.

# PRACTICE

In prayer, invoke the grace of God. Invoke all the powers of healing within you to express themselves, to flood the world with positive vibrations.

Feel and see, looking back over the time you have worked with these readings and practices, how you have been rediscovering yourself. You have come closer to who you are.

See yourself without the slightest blemish of guilt and hurt feelings, without a speck of resentment.

See and experience yourself as truly light in body and mind, with only befriending feelings for everyone. Appreciate and bless every aspect of your life, even the "negatives" of the past, as stepping stones toward befriending your own mind. Feel deep gratitude that God has been so infinitely kind to you by showing you the path to finding your one, true friend.

Beckon that friend of your own heart, the friend who will never leave you, the friend whom not even death can separate from you. This is your most intimate and loving friend, your positive, befriending mind that is in love with God.

Bless all beings on earth. Tell yourself again and again that all is well. Now you are set to experience the bliss of Divine Union, the perennial music of *yoga*, love Divine. Then close with the wonderful Vedic chant for the peace and happiness of all beings:

*Sarve bhavantu sukhinah*
(May all beings in this universe be happy.)
*Sarve santu niramayah*
(May all beings enjoy sound physi-
cal and mental health.)
*Sarve bhadrani pashyantu*
(May we see good and auspiciousness
in each other and in everything.)
*Ma kaschit dukha bhag bhavet*
(May no one be afflicted with mis-
ery and unhappiness.)
*Om Shantihi, Om Shantihi, Om Shantihi.*
(May peace prevail everywhere.)
You may chant this regularly and af-
ter each reading and practice.

# GLOSSARY

Ananda: Pure bliss, extreme happiness, one of the highest states of being or a disciple of Buddha.

Anahat naad: A Hindi word, of Sanskrit origin, it means "primodal sound" in English. The sound that exists and is not produced by striking two objects. This is the sound of the cosmos and of human consciousness, an ultimate sound that transcends space and time, a sound that has no beginning or end.

Ashtavakra: A sage mentioned in Hindu scriptures. He is described as one born with eight different deformities of the body. In Sanskrit, Ashtavakra means "one having eight bends". Ashta means eight, while Vakra means bend or deformity.

Bhakti: Love relationship with Personal God; Devotion to God, Love of God. It is one of the main spiritual disciplines of Hinduism. The devotee loves God with heart and soul, expecting no worldly return from Him.

Buddha: One who has attained Bodhi; and by Bodhi is meant wisdom, an ideal state of intellectual and ethical perfection which can be achieved by man through purely human means. The term Buddha literally means enlightened one, a knower. The Buddha, or Siddhartha Gautama, achieved enlightenment through meditation and his doctrines became the foundation for Buddhism.

Dakshina: A Sanskrit word meaning "Offering in gratitude to the Guru."

Dharma: Duty, law, righteousness, virtue; in Hinduism it denotes the law of inner growth determined by man's actions in his past lives, which influence his present way of live.

Gita: lit. "Song of the Lord", The Bhagavad Gita, often referred to as simply the Gita, is a 700-verse Hindu scripture in Sanskrit that is part of the Hindu epic Mahabharata.

Gunas: The three qualities characterizing the primordial substance, the principal building blocks of nature which bind the embodying self to a particular body. The qualities are Sattwa-purity, harmony; Rajas-emotion, action; Tamas-inertia, darkness.

Guru: The enlightened Master; spiritual preceptor, teacher.

Karma: Action in general; the chain of cause and effect operating in the moral world.

Karma Yoga: The path of Karma Yoga transmutes action into consecration to the Divine. It brings us to the realization that ultimately we are but the instruments of the Universe or the

Divine. The seeker in this path tries to be more and more conscious and aware of the Divine Doer of all actions. The seer and sages tell us "You have rights to the duty but not to the rewards thereof".

King Janaka: Ruler of Mithila and devotee of Ashkravarka.

Maya: Lit. "Illusion". A term of Hindu philosophy denoting ignorance obscuring the vision of reality; the cosmic illusion on account of which the One appears as the many, the Absolute as the relative.

Om Shanti, Om Shanti, Om Shantihi: Peace, Peace, Peace.

Prana: Vital energy

Pranayama: Control of the vital energy (prana) through the practice of breathing exercises.

Raja Yoga: The path of self-discipline and practice. Raja Yoga is also known as Ashtanga Yoga (Eight Steps of Yoga), because it is organised into eight parts: Yama - Self-control. Niyama- Discipline. Asana - Physical exercises._Pranayama - Breath exercises. Pratyahara - Withdrawal of the senses from external objects. Dharana – Concentration. Dhyana – Meditation. Samadhi - Complete Realisation.

Rajasic: Emotion, action

Renunciate:  Any religious devotee who renounces earthly pleasures and lives as an ascetic.

Rishi Patanjali:  The author of the Yoga Sutras and founder of the yoga system, one of the six systems of orthodox Hindu philosophy which deals with control of the mind, meditation, etc.

Sadhana:  The practice of spiritual disciplines.

Samskaras:  An impression or tendency created in the mind of a person as the result of an action or thought. The sum total of a person's samskaras including those from previous births forms his character.

Satguru:  True Guru.  A Divine Incarnation, considered a rare and precious gem that guides both believers and non-believers alike to the Ultimate Goal, to realize the Eternal Reality of All Being One.

Sattwic:  Purity, harmony

Song Celestial:  The Bhagavad Gita.

Shraddha:  Faith in the Truths of the scriptures and in the teachings of the Guru.

Tamasic:  Inertia, darkness

Veda: The most ancient scriptures of the Hindus, regarded by the orthodox as direct divine revelation and supreme authority in all religious matters.

Vishwa-prana: The cosmic breath.

Yadrishi bhavana yashya siddhir bhavati tadrishihi: As you think, so you become.

Yogi: One who is proficient in yoga.

Shuddhaanandaa Brahmachari

# ABOUT THE AUTHOR

SHUDDHAANANDAA BRAHMACHARI IS a globally acclaimed motivational and inspirational speaker, author, spiritual teacher, social advocate and peacemaker. Founder of Stress Management Academy, his Simple Art of Managing Stress and Course in Mindfulness Programs are known worldwide, inspiring corporate leadership, students and spiritual seekers alike.

He is recognized as a visionary social advocate for his development of groundbreaking programs that serve thousands of poverty-stricken individuals in slums of Kolkata, India and remote villages of West Bengal. He founded Lokenath Divine Life Mission in 1985.

His self-authored books include: The Incredible Life of a Himalayan Yogi: The Times, Teachings and Life of Living Shiva Baba Lokenath Brahmachari, Cleaning the Mirror of Mind: Clutter Free Living, Clutter Free Mind, Little Book of Meditation, and The Heart of Meditation Practice.

He has spoken at the Parliament of World Religions, United Nations Global Youth Conference, International Conference of Spiritualizing Leadership, ALL Women's Economic Forum and LIFE (Leadership Initiative for Excellence) Young Leaders Conference. He received a Lifetime Achievement Award from the S.T.A.R foundation at the House of Lords in the United Kingdom on July 21, 2015 for his invaluable and outstanding contribution to society.

www.courseinmindfulness.com

www.facebook.com/srisri.shuddhaanandaa

www.facebook.com/BabaLokenathji